WORDS THAT
CHANGED A NATION

WORDS THAT
CHANGED A NATION

The Most Celebrated and
Influential Speeches of

BARACK OBAMA

pac ps
Pacific Publishing Studio

Published in the United States by Beacon Hill, an imprint of Pacific Publishing Studio.

www.PacPS.com

ISBN – 978-0-9823756-5-5

To order a copy of this book, visit www.Amazon.com.

Special acknowledgement is made to the following:
Introduction: Stacie Vander Pol and WhiteHouse.gov
Cover Photography: Big Stock Photos /
Transcription: Pacific Publishing Studio and WhiteHouse.gov

Table of Contents

Introduction

On January 20, 2009, Barack H. Obama made American history, once again, when he was sworn in as the first African-American President of the United States.

His story is the American story—values from the heartland, a middle-class upbringing in a strong family, hard work and education as the means of getting ahead, and the conviction that a life so blessed should be lived in service to others.

With a father from Kenya and a mother from Kansas, President Obama was born in Hawaii on August 4, 1961. He was raised with help from his grandfather, who served in Patton's army, and his grandmother, who worked her way up from the secretarial pool to middle management at a bank.

After working his way through college with the help of scholarships and student loans, President Obama moved to Chicago, where he worked with a group of churches to help rebuild communities devastated by the closure of local steel plants.

He went on to attend law school, where he became the first African—American president of the *Harvard Law Review*. Upon graduation, he returned to Chicago to help lead a voter registration drive, teach constitutional law at the University of Chicago, and remain active in his community.

President Obama's years of public service are based around his unwavering belief in the ability to unite people around a politics of purpose. In the Illinois State Senate, he passed the first major ethics reform in 25 years, cut taxes for working families, and expanded health care for children and their parents. As a United States Senator, he reached across the aisle to pass groundbreaking lobbying reform, lock up the world's most dangerous weapons, and bring transparency to government by putting federal spending online.

He was elected the 44th President of the United States on November 4, 2008, and sworn in on January 20, 2009.

He and his wife, Michelle, are the proud parents of two daughters, Malia and Sasha.

The Audacity of Hope

Democratic National Convention in Boston
Keynote Address
July 27, 2004

Tonight is a particular honor for me because, let's face it, my presence on this stage is pretty unlikely. My father was a foreign student, born and raised in a small village in Kenya. He grew up herding goats, went to school in a tin-roof shack. His father, my grandfather, was a cook, a domestic servant.

But my grandfather had larger dreams for his son. Through hard work and perseverance, my father got a scholarship to study in a magical place: America, which stood as a beacon of freedom and opportunity to so many who had come before. While studying here, my father met my mother. She was born in a town on the other side of the world, in Kansas. Her father worked on oil rigs and farms through most of the Depression.

The day after Pearl Harbor he signed up for duty, joined Patton's army, and marched across Europe. Back home, my grandmother raised their baby and went to work on a bomber assembly line. After the war, they studied on the GI Bill, bought a house through FHA, and moved west in search of opportunity.

And they, too, had big dreams for their daughter; a common dream born of two continents. My parents shared not only an improbable love; they shared an abiding faith in the possibilities of this nation. They would give me an African name, Barack, or "blessed," believing that in a tolerant America your name is no barrier to success. They imagined me going to the best schools in the land, even though they weren't rich, because in a generous America you don't have to be rich to achieve your potential. They are both passed away now. Yet, I know that on this night they look down on me with pride.

I stand here today, grateful for the diversity of my heritage, aware that my parents' dreams live on in my precious daughters. I stand here knowing that my story is part of the larger American story, that I owe a debt to all of those who came before me, and that in no other country on earth is my story even possible.

Tonight, we gather to affirm the greatness of our nation—not because of the height of our skyscrapers or the power of our military or the size of our economy. Our pride is based on a very simple premise, summed up in a declaration made over two hundred years ago, "We hold these truths to be self-evident, that all men are created equal. That they are endowed by their Creator with certain inalienable rights. That among these are life, liberty and the pursuit of happiness."

That is the true genius of America: a faith in the simple dreams of its people, the insistence on small miracles, that we can tuck in our children at night and know they are fed and clothed and safe from harm. That we can say what we think, write what we think without hearing a sudden knock on the door.

That we can have an idea and start our own business without paying a bribe or hiring somebody's son. That we can participate in the political process without fear of retribution and that our votes will he counted—or at least, most of the time.

This year, in this election, we are called to reaffirm our values and commitments, to hold them against a hard reality and see how we are measuring up to the legacy of our forbearers and the promise of future generations. And fellow Americans— Democrats, Republicans, Independents—I say to you tonight: we have more work to do.

More to do for the workers I met in Galesburg, Illinois, who are losing their union jobs at the Maytag plant that's moving to Mexico and now are having to compete with their own children for jobs that pay seven bucks an hour.

More to do for the father I met who was losing his job and choking back tears, wondering how he would pay $4,500 a month for the drugs his son needs without the health benefits he counted on. More to do for the young woman in East St. Louis, and thousands more like her, who has the grades, has the drive, has the will, but doesn't have the money to go to college.

 Don't get me wrong. The people I meet in small towns and big cities, in diners and office parks, they don't expect government to solve all their problems. They know they have to work hard to get ahead and they want to. Go into the collar counties around Chicago, and people will tell you they don't want their tax money wasted by a welfare agency or the Pentagon.

Go into any inner city neighborhood, and folks will tell you that government alone can't teach kids to learn. They know that parents have to parent, that children can't achieve unless we raise their expectations and turn off the television sets and eradicate the slander that says a black youth with a book is acting white.

No, people don't expect government to solve all their problems. But they sense, deep in their bones, that with just a change in priorities, we can make sure that every child in America has a decent shot at life, and that the doors of opportunity remain open to all. They know we can do better. And they want that choice.

In this election, we offer that choice. Our party has chosen a man to lead us who embodies the best this country has to offer. That man is John Kerry. John Kerry understands the ideals of community, faith, and sacrifice, because they've defined his life. From his heroic service in Vietnam to his years as prosecutor and lieutenant governor, through two decades in the United States Senate, he has devoted himself to this country. Again and again, we've seen him make tough choices when easier ones were available. His values and his record affirm what is best in us.

John Kerry believes in an America where hard work is rewarded. So instead of offering tax breaks to companies shipping jobs overseas, he'll offer them to companies creating jobs here at home. John Kerry believes in an America where all Americans can afford the same health coverage our politicians in Washington have for themselves. John Kerry believes in energy independence, so we aren't held hostage to the profits of oil companies or the sabotage of foreign oil fields.

John Kerry believes in the constitutional freedoms that have made our country the envy of the world, and he will never sacrifice our basic liberties nor use faith as a wedge to divide us. And John Kerry believes that in a dangerous world, war must be an option, but it should never be the first option.

A while back, I met a young man named Shamus at the VFW Hall in East Moline, Illinois. He was a good-looking kid, six-two or six-three, clear-eyed, with an easy smile. He told me he'd joined the Marines and was heading to Iraq the following week.

As I listened to him explain why he'd enlisted, his absolute faith in our country and its leaders, his devotion to duty and service, I thought this young man was all any of us might hope for in a child. But then I asked myself: Are we serving Shamus as well as he was serving us? I thought of more than 900 service men and women, sons and daughters, husbands and wives, friends and neighbors, who will not be returning to their hometowns.

I thought of families I had met who were struggling to get by without a loved one's full income, or whose loved ones had returned with a limb missing or with nerves shattered, but who still lacked long-term health benefits because they were reservists.

When we send our young men and women into harm's way, we have a solemn obligation not to fudge the numbers or shade the truth about why they're going, to care for their families while they're gone, to tend to the soldiers upon their return, and to never ever go to war without enough troops to win the war, secure the peace, and earn the respect of the world.

Now let me be clear. We have real enemies in the world. These enemies must be found. They must be pursued and they must be defeated. John Kerry knows this. And just as Lieutenant Kerry did not hesitate to risk his life to protect the men who served with him in Vietnam, President Kerry will not hesitate one moment to use our military might to keep America safe and secure.

John Kerry believes in America. And he knows it's not enough for just some of us to prosper. For alongside our famous individualism, there's another ingredient in the American saga.

A belief that we are connected as one people. If there's a child on the south side of Chicago who can't read, that matters to me, even if it's not my child. If there's a senior citizen somewhere who can't pay for her prescription and has to choose between medicine and the rent, that makes my life poorer, even if it's not my grandmother. If there's an Arab American family being rounded up without benefit of an attorney or due process, that threatens my civil liberties.

It's that fundamental belief—I am my brother's keeper, I am my sister's keeper—that makes this country work.

It's what allows us to pursue our individual dreams, yet still come together as a single American family. "E pluribus unum." Out of many, one.

Yet even as we speak, there are those who are preparing to divide us, the spin masters and negative ad peddlers who embrace the politics of anything goes. Well, I say to them tonight, there's not a liberal America and a conservative America—there's the United States of America.

There's not a black America and white America and Latino America and Asian America; there's the United States of America. The pundits like to slice-and-dice our country into red states and blue states; red states for Republicans, blue states for Democrats. But I've got news for them, too. We worship an awesome God in the blue states, and we don't like federal agents poking around our libraries in the red states.

THE VOICE THAT CHANGED A NATION

We coach little league in the blue states and have gay friends in the red states.

There are patriots who opposed the war in Iraq and patriots who supported it. We are one people, all of us pledging allegiance to the stars and stripes, all of us defending the United States of America.

In the end, that's what this election is about. Do we participate in a politics of cynicism or a politics of hope? John Kerry calls on us to hope. John Edwards calls on us to hope. I'm not talking about blind optimism here—the almost willful ignorance that thinks unemployment will go away if we just don't talk about it, or the health care crisis will solve itself if we just ignore it. No, I'm talking about something more substantial.

It's the hope of slaves sitting around a fire singing freedom songs, the hope of immigrants setting out for distant shores, the hope of a young naval lieutenant bravely patrolling the Mekong Delta, the hope of a millworker's son who dares to defy the odds, the hope of a skinny kid with a funny name who believes that America has a place for him, too.

The audacity of hope!

In the end, that is God's greatest gift to us, the bedrock of this nation—the belief in things not seen, the belief that there are better days ahead. I believe we can give our middle class relief and provide working families with a road to opportunity.

I believe we can provide jobs to the jobless, homes to the homeless, and reclaim young people in cities across America from violence and despair. I believe that as we stand on the crossroads of history, we can make the right choices, and meet the challenges that face us. America!

Tonight, if you feel the same energy I do, the same urgency I do, the same passion I do, the same hopefulness I do—if we do what we must do, then I have no doubt that all across the country, from Florida to Oregon, from Washington to Maine, the people will rise up in November, and John Kerry will be sworn in as president, and John Edwards will be sworn in as vice president, and this country will reclaim its promise. And out of this long political darkness a brighter day will come.

Thank you and God bless you.

Take Back America

Take Back America Conference
Washington, DC
June 14, 2006

My friends, we meet here today at a time where we find ourselves at a crossroads in America's history.

It's a time where you can go to any town hall or street corner or coffee shop and hear people express the same anxiety about the future—hear them convey the same uncertainty about the direction we're headed as a country. Whether it's the war or Katrina or their health care or their jobs, you hear people say that we've finally arrived at a moment where something must change.

These are Americans who still believe in an America where anything's possible—they just don't think their leaders do. These are Americans who still dream big dreams—they just sense their leaders have forgotten how.

I remember when I first ran for the State Senate—my very first race. A seat had opened up and some friends asked me if I'd be interested in running. Well, I thought about it, and then I did what every wise man does when faced with a difficult decision: I prayed, and I asked my wife.

And after consulting with these higher powers, I threw my hat in the ring and I did what every person on a campaign does—I talked to anyone who'd listen.

I went to bake sales and barber shops, and if there were two guys standing on the corner, I'd pull up and hand them literature. And everywhere I went I'd get two questions:

First, they'd ask, "Where'd you get that funny name, Barack Obama?" Because people just couldn't pronounce it. They'd call me "Alabama," or they'd call me "Yo Mama." And I'd have to explain that I got the name from my father, who was from Kenya.

And the second thing people would ask me was, "You seem like a nice young man. You teach law school, you're a civil rights attorney, you organize voter registration, you're a family man. Why would you want to go into something dirty and nasty like politics?"

And I understood the question because it revealed the cynicism people feel about public life today. That even though we may get involved out of civic obligation every few years, we don't always have confidence that government can make a difference in our lives.

So I understand the cynicism. But whenever I get in that mood, I think about something that happened to me on the eve of my election to the United States Senate.

We had held a large rally the night before in the Southside of Chicago, which is where I live. And in the midst of this rally, someone comes up to me and says that there's a woman who'd like to come meet you, and she's traveled a long way and she wants to take a picture and shake your hand.

And so I said fine and I met her and we talked.

And all of this would have been unremarkable except for the fact that this woman, Marguerite Lewis, was born in 1899 and was 105 years old.

And ever since I met this frail, 105 year old African-American woman who had found the strength to leave her house and come to a rally because she believed that her voice mattered.

I've thought about all she's seen in her life. I've thought about the fact that when she was born, there weren't cars on the road and no airplanes in the sky. That she was born under the cloud of Jim Crow, free in theory but still enslaved in so many ways. That she was born at a time for black folks when lynchings were not uncommon, but voting was.

I've thought about how she lived to see a world war and a Great Depression and a second world war, and how she saw her brothers and uncles and nephews and cousins coming home from those wars and still have to sit at the back of a bus.

And I thought about how she saw women finally win the right to vote. And how she watched FDR lift this nation out of fear and send millions to college on the GI Bill and lift millions out of poverty with Social Security. How she saw unions rise up and a middle-class prosper, and watched immigrants leave distant shores in search of an idea known as America.

She believed in this idea with all her heart, and she saw this progress around her and she had faith that someday it would be her turn. And when she finally saw hope breaking through the horizon in the Civil Rights Movement, she thought, "Maybe it's my turn."

And in that movement, she saw women who were willing to walk instead of ride the bus after a day of doing somebody else's laundry and looking after somebody else's children because they walked for freedom. And she saw young people of every race and every creed take a bus down to Mississippi and Alabama to register voters because they believed. She saw four little girls die in a Sunday school and catalyze a nation.

And at last—at last—she saw the passage of the Civil Rights Act and the Voting Rights Act.

And she saw people lining up to vote for the first time—and she got in that line—and she never forgot it. She kept on voting in each and every election because she believed. She believed that over a span of three centuries, she had seen enough to know that there is no challenge too great, no injustice too crippling, no destiny too far out of reach for America.

She believed that we don't have to settle for equality for some, or opportunity for the lucky, or freedom for the few.

And she knew that during those moments in history where it looked like we might give up hope or settle for less, there have always been Americans who refused—who said we're going to keep on dreaming, and we're going to keep on building, and we're going to keep on marching, and we're going to keep on working because that's who we are. Because we've always fought to bring all of our people under the blanket of the American Dream.

And I think that we face one of those moments today.

In a century just six years old, our faith has been shaken by war and terror, disaster and despair, threats to the middle-class dream, and scandal and corruption in our government.

The sweeping changes brought by revolutions in technology have torn down walls between business and government and people and places all over the globe. And with this new world comes new risks and new dangers.

No longer can we assume that a high school education is enough to compete for a job that could easily go to a college educated student in Bangalore or Beijing. No more can we count on employers to provide health care and pensions and job training when their bottom lines know no borders. Never again can we expect the oceans that surround America to keep us safe from attacks on our own soil.

The world has changed. And as a result, we've seen families work harder for less and our jobs go overseas. We've seen the cost of health care and child care and gasoline skyrocket. We've seen our children leave for Iraq and terrorists threaten to finish the job they started on 9/11.

But while the world has changed around us, too often our government has stood still. Our faith has been shaken, but the people running Washington aren't willing to make us believe again.

It's the timidity, the smallness of our politics that's holding us back right now. The idea that some problems are just too big to handle, and if you just ignore them, sooner or later, they'll go away.

That if you give a speech where you rattle off statistics about the stock market being up and orders for durable goods being on the rise, no one will notice the single mom whose two jobs won't pay the bills or the student who can't afford his college dreams.

That if you say the words "plan for victory" and point to the number of schools painted and roads paved and cell phones used in Iraq, no one will notice the nearly 2,500 flag-draped coffins that have arrived at Dover Air Force base.

Well, it's time we finally said we notice and we care, and we're not going to settle anymore.

You know, you probably never thought you'd hear this at a Take Back America conference, but Newt Gingrich made a great point a few weeks ago. He was talking about what an awful job his own party has done governing this country, and he said that with all the mistakes and misjudgments the Republicans have made over the last six years, the slogan for the Democrats should come down to just two words:

Had enough?

I don't know about you, but I think old Newt is onto something here. Because I think we've all had enough. Enough of the broken promises. Enough of the failed leadership. Enough of the can't do, won't do, won't even try style of governance.

Four years after 9/11, I've had enough of being told that we can find the money to give Paris Hilton more tax cuts, but we can't find enough to protect our ports or our railroads or our chemical plants or our borders.

I've had enough of the closed-door deals that give billions to the HMOs when we're told that we can't do a thing for the 45

THE VOICE THAT CHANGED A NATION

million uninsured or the millions more who can't pay their medical bills.

I've had enough of being told that we can't afford body armor for our troops and health care for our veterans and benefits for the wounded heroes who've risked their lives for this country. I've had enough of that.

I've had enough of giving billions away to the oil companies when we're told that we can't invest in the renewable energy that will create jobs and lower gas prices and finally free us from our dependence on the oil wells of Saudi Arabia.

I've had enough of our kids going to schools where the rats outnumber the computers. I've had enough of Katrina survivors living out of their cars and begging FEMA for trailers. And I've had enough of being told that all we can do about this is sit and wait and hope that the good fortune of a few trickles on down to everyone else in this country.

You know, we all remember that George Bush said in 2000 that he was against nation building. We just didn't know he was talking about this one.

Now, let me say this—I don't think that George Bush is a bad man. I think he loves his country. I don't think this administration is full of stupid people. I think there are a lot of smart folks in there. The problem isn't that their philosophy isn't working the way it's supposed to—it's that it is. It's that it's doing exactly what it's supposed to do.

The reason they don't believe government has a role in solving national problems is because they think government is the problem. That we're better off if we dismantle it—if we divvy it up into individual tax breaks, hand them out, and encourage everyone to go buy your own health care, your own retirement security, your own child care, their own schools, your own private security force, your own roads, their own levees.

It's called the Ownership Society in Washington. But in our past there has been another term for it—Social Darwinism—every man or women for him or herself.

It allows us to say to those whose health care or tuition may rise faster than they can afford—life isn't fair. It allows us to say to the child who didn't have the foresight to choose the right parents or be born in the right suburb—pick yourself up by your bootstraps. It lets us say to the guy who worked twenty or thirty years in the factory and then watched his plant move out to Mexico or China—we're sorry, but you're on your own.

It's a bracing idea. It's a tempting idea. And it's the easiest thing in the world.

But there's just one problem. It doesn't work. It ignores our history. Yes, our greatness as a nation has depended on individual initiative, on a belief in the free market. But it has also depended on our sense of mutual regard for each other, of mutual responsibility. The idea that everybody has a stake in the country, that we're all in it together, and everybody's got a shot at opportunity.

Americans know this. We know that government can't solve all our problems—and we don't want it to.

But we also know that there are some things we can't do on our own. We know that there are some things we do better together.

We know that we've been called in churches and mosques, synagogues and Sunday schools to love our neighbors as ourselves; to be our brother's keeper, to be our sister's keeper. That we have individual responsibility, but we also have collective responsibility to each other.

That's what America is.

And so I am eager to have this argument not just with the President, but the entire Republican Party over what this country is about.

Because I think that this is our moment to lead.

The time for our party's identity crisis is over. Don't let anyone tell you we don't know what we stand for, and don't doubt it yourselves. We know who we are. And in the end, we know that it isn't enough to just say that you've had enough.

So let it be said that we are the party of opportunity. That in a global economy that's more connected and more competitive—we are the party that will guarantee every American an affordable, world-class, top-notch, life-long education—from early childhood to high school, from college to on-the-job training.

Let it be said that we are the party of affordable, accessible health care for all Americans. The party that won't make Americans choose between a health care plan that bankrupts the government and one that bankrupts families. The party that won't just throw a few tax breaks at families who can't afford their insurance, but modernizes our health care system and gives every family a chance to buy insurance at a price they can afford.

Let it be said that we are the party of an energy independent America. The party that's not bought and paid for by the oil companies. The party that will harness homegrown, alternative fuels and spur the production of fuel-efficient, hybrid cars to break our dependence on the world's most dangerous regimes.

Let it be said that we will conduct a smart foreign policy that battles the forces of terrorism and fundamentalism wherever they may exist by matching the might of our military with the power of our diplomacy and the strength of our alliances. And when we do go to war, let us always be honest with the American people about why we are there and how we will win.

And let it be said that we are the party of open, honest government that doesn't peddle the agenda of whichever lobbyist or special interest can write the biggest check. The party who believes that in this democracy, influence and access should begin and end with the power of the ballot.

If we do all this, if we can be trusted to lead, this will not be a Democratic Agenda, it will be an American agenda. Because in the end, we may be proud Democrats, but we are prouder Americans. We're tired of being divided, tired of running into ideological walls and partisan roadblocks, tired of appeals to our worst instincts and greatest fears.

Americans everywhere are desperate for leadership. They are longing for direction. And they want to believe again. A while ago, I was reading through Jonathan Kozol's new book, Shame of a Nation, which tells of his travels to underprivileged schools across America.

At one point, Kozol tells about his trip to Fremont High School in Los Angeles, where he met a girl who tells him that she'd

THE VOICE THAT CHANGED A NATION

taken hairdressing twice, because there were actually two different levels offered by the high school. The first was in hairstyling, the other in braiding.

Another girl, Mireya, listened as her friend told this story. And she began to cry. When asked what was wrong, she said, "I don't want to take hairdressing. I did not need sewing either. I knew how to sew. My mother is a seamstress in a factory. I'm trying to go to college. I don't need to sew to go to college. My mother sews. I hoped for something else."

I hoped for something else.

I've often thought about Mireya and her simple dream and all those before her who've shared that dream too.

And I've wondered—if she is lucky enough to live as long as 105 year old Marguerite Lewis, if she someday has the chance to look back across the twenty-first century, what will she see? Will she see a country that is freer and kinder, more tolerant and more just than the one she grew up in? Will she see greater opportunities for every citizen of this country? Will all her childhood hopes be fulfilled?

We are here tonight because we believe that in this country, we have it within our power to say "yes" to those questions— to forge our own destiny—to begin the world anew.

Ladies and gentlemen, this is our time. Our time to make a mark on history. Our time to write a new chapter in the American story. Our time to leave our children a country that is freer and kinder, more prosperous and more just than the place we grew up.

And then someday, someday, if our kids get the chance to stand where we are and look back at the beginning of the 21st century, they can say that this was the time when America renewed its purpose.

They can say that this was the time when America found its way.

They can say that this was the time when America learned to dream again.

Our Past, Future, and Vision for America

Presidential Candidacy Announcement
Springfield, Illinois
February 10, 2007

Let me begin by saying thanks to all you who've traveled from far-and-wide, to brave the cold today.

We all made this journey for a reason. It's humbling, but in my heart I know you didn't come here just for me, you came here because you believe in what this country can be.

In the face of war, you believe there can be peace. In the face of despair, you believe there can be hope. In the face of a politics that's shut you out, that's told you to settle, that's divided us for too long, you believe we can be one people reaching for what's possible, building that more perfect union.

That's the journey we're on today. But let me tell you how I came to be here. As most of you know, I am not a native of this great state. I moved to Illinois over two decades ago. I was a young man then, just a year out of college. I knew no one in Chicago, was without money or family connections. But a group of churches had offered me a job as a community organizer for $13,000 a year. And I accepted the job, sight unseen, motivated then by a single, simple, powerful idea that I might play a small part in building a better America.

My work took me to some of Chicago's poorest neighborhoods. I joined with pastors and lay-people to deal with communities that had been ravaged by plant closings. I saw that the problems people faced weren't simply local in nature—that the decision to close a steel mill was made by distant executives—that the lack of textbooks and computers in schools could be traced to the skewed priorities of politicians a thousand miles away—and that when a child turns to violence, there's a hole in his heart no government could ever fill.

It was in these neighborhoods that I received the best education I ever had and where I learned the true meaning of my Christian faith.

After three years of this work, I went to law school because I wanted to understand how the law should work for those in need. I became a civil rights lawyer and taught constitutional law. And after a time, I came to understand that our cherished rights of liberty and equality depend on the active participation of an awakened electorate. It was with these ideas in mind that I arrived in this capital city as a State Senator.

It was here, in Springfield, where I saw all that is America converge—farmers and teachers, businessmen and laborers—all of them with a story to tell, all of them seeking a seat at the table, all of them clamoring to be heard. I made lasting friendships here—friends that I see in the audience today.

It was here we learned to disagree without being disagreeable—that it's possible to compromise so long as you know those principles that can never be compromised; and that so long as we're willing to listen to each other, we can assume the best in people instead of the worst.

THE VOICE THAT CHANGED A NATION

That's why we were able to reform a death penalty system that was broken. That's why we were able to give health insurance to children in need. That's why we made the tax system more fair and just for working families. And that's why we passed ethics reforms that the cynics said could never, ever be passed.

It was here, in Springfield, where North, South, East, and West come together that I was reminded of the essential decency of the American people—where I came to believe that through this decency, we can build a more hopeful America.

And that is why, in the shadow of the Old State Capitol, where Lincoln once called on a divided house to stand together, where common hopes and common dreams still, I stand before you today to announce my candidacy for President of the United States.

I recognize there is a certain presumptuousness—a certain audacity—to this announcement. I know I haven't spent a lot of time learning the ways of Washington. But I've been there long enough to know that the ways of Washington must change.

The genius of our founders is that they designed a system of government that can be changed. And we should take heart, because we've changed this country before. In the face of tyranny, a band of patriots brought an Empire to its knees.

In the face of secession, we unified a nation and set the captives free. In the face of Depression, we put people back to work and lifted millions out of poverty. We welcomed immigrants to our shores, we opened railroads to the west, we landed a man on the moon, and we heard a King's call to let justice roll down like water, and righteousness like a mighty stream.

Each and every time, a new generation has risen up and done what's needed to be done.

Today, we are called once more. And it is time for our generation to answer that call.

For that is our unyielding faith—that in the face of impossible odds, people who love their country can change it.

That's what Abraham Lincoln understood. He had his doubts. He had his defeats. He had his setbacks. But through his will and his words, he moved a nation and helped free a people. It is because of the millions who rallied to his cause that we are no longer divided, North and South, slave and free.

It is because men and women of every race, from every walk of life continued to march for freedom long after Lincoln was laid to rest—that today we have the chance to face the challenges of this millennium together, as one people, as Americans.

All of us know what those challenges are today—a war with no end, a dependence on oil that threatens our future, schools where too many children aren't learning, and families struggling paycheck to paycheck despite working as hard as they can. We know the challenges. We've heard them. We've talked about them for years.

What's stopped us from meeting these challenges is not the absence of sound policies and sensible plans. What's stopped us is the failure of leadership, the smallness of our politics—the ease with which we're distracted by the petty and trivial, our chronic avoidance of tough decisions, our preference for scoring cheap political points instead of rolling up our sleeves and building a working consensus to tackle big problems.

For the last six years we've been told that our mounting debts don't matter, we've been told that the anxiety Americans feel about rising health care costs and stagnant wages are an illusion, we've been told that climate change is a hoax, and that tough talk and an ill-conceived war can replace diplomacy, and strategy, and foresight. And when all else fails, when Katrina happens, or the death toll in Iraq mounts, we've been told that our crises are somebody else's fault.

We're distracted from our real failures, and told to blame the other party, or gay people, or immigrants.

And as people have looked away in disillusionment and frustration, we know what's filled the void. The cynics, and the lobbyists, and the special interests who've turned our government into a game only they can afford to play. They write the checks and you get stuck with the bills, they get the access while you get to write a letter, they think they own this government, but we're here today to take it back. The time for that politics is over. It's time to turn the page.

We've made some progress already. I was proud to help lead the fight in Congress that led to the most sweeping ethics reform since Watergate.

But Washington has a long way to go. And it won't be easy. That's why we'll have to set priorities. We'll have to make hard choices. And although government will play a crucial role in bringing about the changes we need, more money and programs alone will not get us where we need to go.

Each of us, in our own lives, will have to accept responsibility—for instilling an ethic of achievement in our children, for adapting to a more competitive economy, for strengthening our communities, and sharing some measure of sacrifice. So let us begin. Let us begin this hard work together. Let us transform this nation.

Let us be the generation that reshapes our economy to compete in the digital age. Let's set high standards for our schools and give them the resources they need to succeed. Let's recruit a new army of teachers, and give them better pay and more support in exchange for more accountability. Let's make college more affordable, and let's invest in scientific research, and let's lay down broadband lines through the heart of inner cities and rural towns all across America.

And as our economy changes, let's be the generation that ensures our nation's workers are sharing in our prosperity. Let's protect the hard-earned benefits their companies have promised. Let's make it possible for hardworking Americans to save for retirement. And let's allow our unions and their organizers to lift up this country's middle-class again.

Let's be the generation that ends poverty in America. Every single person willing to work should be able to get job training that leads to a job, and earn a living wage that can pay the bills, and afford child care so their kids have a safe place to go when they work. Let's do this.

Let's be the generation that finally tackles our health care crisis. We can control costs by focusing on prevention, by providing better treatment to the chronically ill, and using technology to cut the bureaucracy. Let's be the generation that says right here, right now, that we will have universal health care in America by the end of the next president's first term.

THE VOICE THAT CHANGED A NATION

Let's be the generation that finally frees America from the tyranny of oil. We can harness homegrown, alternative fuels like ethanol and spur the production of more fuel-efficient cars. We can set up a system for capping greenhouse gases. We can turn this crisis of global warming into a moment of opportunity for innovation, and job creation, and an incentive for businesses that will serve as a model for the world.

Let's be the generation that makes future generations proud of what we did here.

Most of all, let's be the generation that never forgets what happened on that September day and confront the terrorists with everything we've got. Politics doesn't have to divide us on this anymore—we can work together to keep our country safe. I've worked with Republican Senator Dick Lugar to pass a law that will secure and destroy some of the world's deadliest, unguarded weapons. We can work together to track terrorists down with a stronger military, we can tighten the net around their finances, and we can improve our intelligence capabilities. But let us also understand that ultimate victory against our enemies will come only by rebuilding our alliances and exporting those ideals that bring hope and opportunity to millions around the globe.

But all of this cannot come to pass until we bring an end to this war in Iraq. Most of you know I opposed this war from the start. I thought it was a tragic mistake. Today we grieve for the families who have lost loved ones, the hearts that have been broken, and the young lives that could have been.

America, it's time to start bringing our troops home. It's time to admit that no amount of American lives can resolve the political disagreement that lies at the heart of someone else's civil war. That's why I have a plan that will bring our combat troops home by March of 2008. Letting the Iraqis know that we will not be there forever is our last, best hope to pressure the Sunni and Shia to come to the table and find peace.

Finally, there is one other thing that is not too late to get right about this war—and that is the homecoming of the men and women-our veterans-who have sacrificed the most. Let us honor their valor by providing the care they need and rebuilding the military they love. Let us be the generation that begins this work.

I know there are those who don't believe we can do all these things. I understand the skepticism. After all, every four years, candidates from both parties make similar promises, and I expect this year will be no different. All of us running for president will travel around the country offering ten-point plans and making grand speeches; all of us will trumpet those qualities we believe make us uniquely qualified to lead the country.

But too many times, after the election is over, and the confetti is swept away, all those promises fade from memory, and the lobbyists and the special interests move in, and people turn away, disappointed as before, left to struggle on their own.

That is why this campaign can't only be about me. It must be about us—it must be about what we can do together. This campaign must be the occasion, the vehicle, of your hopes, and your dreams. It will take your time, your energy, and your advice—to push us forward when we're doing right, and to let us know when we're not.

This campaign has to be about reclaiming the meaning of citizenship, restoring our sense of common purpose, and realizing that few obstacles can withstand the power of millions of voices calling for change.

By ourselves, this change will not happen. Divided, we are bound to fail.

But the life of a tall, gangly, self-made Springfield lawyer tells us that a different future is possible. He tells us that there is power in words. He tells us that there is power in conviction. That beneath all the differences of race and region, faith and station, we are one people.

He tells us that there is power in hope.

As Lincoln organized the forces arrayed against slavery, he was heard to say: "Of strange, discordant, and even hostile elements, we gathered from the four winds, and formed and fought to battle through."

That is our purpose here today. That's why I'm in this race. Not just to hold an office, but to gather with you to transform a nation. I want to win that next battle—for justice and opportunity.

I want to win that next battle—for better schools, and better jobs, and health care for all. I want us to take up the unfinished business of perfecting our union, and building a better America.

And if you will join me in this improbable quest, if you feel destiny calling, and see as I see, a future of endless possibility stretching before us; if you sense, as I sense, that the time is now to shake off our slumber, and slough off our fear, and make good on the debt we owe past and future generations, then I'm ready to take up the cause, and march with you, and work with you.

Together, starting today, let us finish the work that needs to be done, and usher in a new birth of freedom on this Earth.

Yes We Can

South Carolina Victory Speech
Columbia, South Carolina
January 26, 2008

Over two weeks ago, we saw the people of Iowa proclaim that our time for change has come. But there were those who doubted this country's desire for something new—who said Iowa was a fluke not to be repeated again.

Well, tonight, the cynics who believed that what began in the snows of Iowa was just an illusion were told a different story by the good people of South Carolina.

After four great contests in every corner of this country, we have the most votes, the most delegates, and the most diverse coalition of Americans we've seen in a long, long time.

They are young and old; rich and poor. They are black and white; Latino and Asian. They are Democrats from Des Moines and Independents from Concord; Republicans from rural Nevada and young people across this country who've never had a reason to participate until now. And in nine days, nearly half the nation will have the chance to join us in saying that we are tired of business-as-usual in Washington, we are hungry for change, and we are ready to believe again.

But if there's anything we've been reminded of since Iowa, it's that the kind of change we seek will not come easy. Partly because we have fine candidates in the field—fierce

31

competitors, worthy of respect. And as contentious as this campaign may get, we have to remember that this is a contest for the Democratic nomination, and that all of us share an abiding desire to end the disastrous policies of the current administration.

But there are real differences between the candidates. We are looking for more than just a change of party in the White House. We're looking to fundamentally change the status quo in Washington—a status quo that extends beyond any particular party.

And right now, that status quo is fighting back with everything it's got; with the same old tactics that divide and distract us from solving the problems people face, whether those problems are health care they can't afford or a mortgage they cannot pay.

So this will not be easy. Make no mistake about what we're up against.

We are up against the belief that it's ok for lobbyists to dominate our government—that they are just part of the system in Washington. But we know that the undue influence of lobbyists is part of the problem, and this election is our chance to say that we're not going to let them stand in our way anymore.

 We are up against the conventional thinking that says your ability to lead as President comes from longevity in Washington or proximity to the White House. But we know that real leadership is about candor, and judgment, and the ability to rally Americans from all walks of life around a common purpose—a higher purpose.

We are up against decades of bitter partisanship that cause politicians to demonize their opponents instead of coming together to make college affordable or energy cleaner; it's the kind of partisanship where you're not even allowed to say that a Republican had an idea—even if it's one you never agreed with. That kind of politics is bad for our party, it's bad for our country, and this is our chance to end it once and for all.

We are up against the idea that it's acceptable to say anything and do anything to win an election. We know that this is exactly what's wrong with our politics; this is why people don't believe what their leaders say anymore; this is why they tune out. And this election is our chance to give the American people a reason to believe again.

And what we've seen in these last weeks is that we're also up against forces that are not the fault of any one campaign, but feed the habits that prevent us from being who we want to be as a nation. It's the politics that uses religion as a wedge, and patriotism as a bludgeon. A politics that tells us that we have to think, act, and even vote within the confines of the categories that supposedly define us.

The assumption that young people are apathetic. The assumption that Republicans won't cross over. The assumption that the wealthy care nothing for the poor, and that the poor don't vote. The assumption that African-Americans can't support the white candidate; whites can't support the African-American candidate; blacks and Latinos can't come together.

But we are here tonight to say that this is not the America we believe in. I did not travel around this state over the last year and see a white South Carolina or a black South Carolina. I saw South Carolina. I saw crumbling schools that are stealing the future of black children and white children.

I saw shuttered mills and homes for sale that once belonged to Americans from all walks of life, and men and women of every color and creed who serve together, and fight together, and bleed together under the same proud flag. I saw what America is, and I believe in what this country can be.

That is the country I see. That is the country you see. But now it is up to us to help the entire nation embrace this vision. Because in the end, we are not just up against the ingrained and destructive habits of Washington, we are also struggling against our own doubts, our own fears, and our own cynicism.

The change we seek has always required great struggle and sacrifice. And so this is a battle in our own hearts and minds about what kind of country we want and how hard we're willing to work for it.

So let me remind you tonight that change will not be easy. That change will take time. There will be setbacks, and false starts, and sometimes we will make mistakes. But as hard as it may seem, we cannot lose hope. Because there are people all across this country who are counting us; who can't afford another four years without health care or good schools or decent wages because our leaders couldn't come together and get it done.

Theirs are the stories and voices we carry on from South Carolina.

The mother who can't get Medicaid to cover all the needs of her sick child—she needs us to pass a health care plan that cuts costs and makes health care available and affordable for every single American.

The teacher who works another shift at Dunkin Donuts after school just to make ends meet—she needs us to reform our education system so that she gets better pay, and more support, and her students get the resources they need to achieve their dreams.

The Maytag worker who is now competing with his own teenager for a $7-an-hour job at Wal-Mart because the factory he gave his life to shut its doors—he needs us to stop giving tax breaks to companies that ship our jobs overseas and start putting them in the pockets of working Americans who deserve it. And struggling homeowners. And seniors who should retire with dignity and respect.

The woman who told me that she hasn't been able to breathe since the day her nephew left for Iraq, or the soldier who doesn't know his child because he's on his third or fourth tour of duty—they need us to come together and put an end to a war that should've never been authorized and never been waged.

The choice in this election is not between regions or religions or genders. It's not about rich versus poor; young versus old; and it is not about black versus white.

It's about the past versus the future.

It's about whether we settle for the same divisions and distractions and drama that passes for politics today, or whether we reach for a politics of common sense, and innovation—a shared sacrifice and shared prosperity.

There are those who will continue to tell us we cannot do this. That we cannot have what we long for. That we are peddling false hopes.

But here's what I know. I know that when people say we can't overcome all the big money and influence in Washington, I think of the elderly woman who sent me a contribution the other day—an envelope that had a money order for $3.01 along with a verse of scripture tucked inside. So don't tell us change isn't possible.

When I hear the cynical talk that blacks and whites and Latinos can't join together and work together, I'm reminded of the Latino brothers and sisters I organized with, and stood with, and fought with side by side for jobs and justice on the streets of Chicago. So don't tell us change can't happen.

When I hear that we'll never overcome the racial divide in our politics, I think about that Republican woman who used to work for Strom Thurmond, who's now devoted to educating inner-city children and who went out onto the streets of South Carolina and knocked on doors for this campaign. Don't tell me we can't change.

Yes we can change.

Yes we can heal this nation.

Yes we can seize our future.

And as we leave this state with a new wind at our backs, and take this journey across the country we love with the message we've carried from the plains of Iowa to the hills of New Hampshire; from the Nevada desert to the South Carolina coast; the same message we had when we were up and when we were down—that out of many, we are one; that while we breathe, we hope; and where we are met with cynicism, and doubt, and those who tell us that we can't, we will respond with that timeless creed that sums up the spirit of a people in three simple words:

Yes. We. Can.

A More Perfect Union

Including Comments on Revered Wright
Philadelphia, PA
March 18, 2008

"We the people, in order to form a more perfect union..."

Two hundred and twenty one years ago, in a hall that still stands across the street, a group of men gathered and, with these simple words, launched America's improbable experiment in democracy. Farmers and scholars, statesmen and patriots, who had traveled across an ocean to escape tyranny and persecution, finally made real their declaration of independence at a Philadelphia convention that lasted through the spring of 1787.

The document they produced was eventually signed but ultimately unfinished. It was stained by this nation's original sin of slavery, a question that divided the colonies and brought the convention to a stalemate until the founders chose to allow the slave trade to continue for at least twenty more years, and to leave any final resolution to future generations.

Of course, the answer to the slavery question was already embedded within our Constitution—a Constitution that had at its very core the ideal of equal citizenship under the law; a Constitution that promised its people liberty and justice, and a union that could be and should be perfected over time.

And yet words on a parchment would not be enough to deliver slaves from bondage, or provide men and women of every color and creed their full rights and obligations as citizens of the United States. What would be needed were Americans in successive generations who were willing to do their part—through protests and struggle, on the streets and in the courts, through a civil war and civil disobedience, and always at great risk—to narrow that gap between the promise of our ideals and the reality of their time.

This was one of the tasks we set forth at the beginning of this campaign—to continue the long march of those who came before us, a march for a more just, more equal, more free, more caring, and more prosperous America.

I chose to run for the presidency at this moment in history because I believe deeply that we cannot solve the challenges of our time unless we solve them together—unless we perfect our union by understanding that we may have different stories, but we hold common hopes; that we may not look the same and we may not have come from the same place, but we all want to move in the same direction—towards a better future for our children and our grandchildren.

This belief comes from my unyielding faith in the decency and generosity of the American people. But it also comes from my own American story.

I am the son of a black man from Kenya and a white woman from Kansas. I was raised with the help of a white grandfather who survived a Depression to serve in Patton's Army during World War II, and a white grandmother who worked on a bomber assembly line at Fort Leavenworth while he was overseas. I've gone to some of the best schools in America and lived in one of the world's poorest nations.

38   *THE VOICE THAT CHANGED A NATION*

I am married to a black American who carries within her the blood of slaves and slave owners—an inheritance we pass on to our two precious daughters. I have brothers, sisters, nieces, nephews, uncles, and cousins of every race and every hue— scattered across three continents. And for as long as I live, I will never forget that in no other country on Earth is my story even possible.

It's a story that hasn't made me the most conventional candidate. But it is a story that has seared into my genetic makeup the idea that this nation is more than the sum of its parts—that out of many, we are truly one.

Throughout the first year of this campaign, against all predictions to the contrary, we saw how hungry the American people were for this message of unity. Despite the temptation to view my candidacy through a purely racial lens, we won commanding victories in states with some of the whitest populations in the country. In South Carolina, where the Confederate Flag still flies, we built a powerful coalition of African Americans and white Americans.

This is not to say that race has not been an issue in the campaign. At various stages in the campaign, some commentators have deemed me either "too black" or "not black enough." We saw racial tensions bubble to the surface during the week before the South Carolina primary. The press has scoured every exit poll for the latest evidence of racial polarization, not just in terms of white and black, but black and brown as well.

And yet, it has only been in the last couple of weeks that the discussion of race in this campaign has taken a particularly divisive turn.

On one end of the spectrum, we've heard the implication that my candidacy is somehow an exercise in affirmative action; that it's based solely on the desire of wide-eyed liberals to purchase racial reconciliation on the cheap. On the other end, we've heard my former pastor, Reverend Jeremiah Wright, use incendiary language to express views that have the potential not only to widen the racial divide, but views that denigrate both the greatness and the goodness of our nation—that rightly offend white and black alike.

I have already condemned, in unequivocal terms, the statements of Reverend Wright that have caused such controversy. For some, nagging questions remain. Did I know him to be an occasionally fierce critic of American domestic and foreign policy? Of course. Did I ever hear him make remarks that could be considered controversial while I sat in church? Yes. Did I strongly disagree with many of his political views? Absolutely—just as I'm sure many of you have heard remarks from your pastors, priests, or rabbis with which you strongly disagreed.

But the remarks that have caused this recent firestorm weren't simply controversial. They weren't simply a religious leader's effort to speak out against perceived injustice. Instead, they expressed a profoundly distorted view of this country—a view that sees white racism as endemic, and that elevates what is wrong with America above all that we know is right with America; a view that sees the conflicts in the Middle East as rooted primarily in the actions of stalwart allies like Israel, instead of emanating from the perverse and hateful ideologies of radical Islam.

As such, Reverend Wright's comments were not only wrong but divisive, divisive at a time when we need unity; racially charged at a time when we need to come together to solve a

40   *THE VOICE THAT CHANGED A NATION*

set of monumental problems: two wars, a terrorist threat, a falling economy, a chronic health care crisis, and potentially devastating climate change; problems that are neither black or white or Latino or Asian, but rather problems that confront us all.

Given my background, my politics, and my professed values and ideals, there will no doubt be those for whom my statements of condemnation are not enough. Why associate myself with Reverend Wright in the first place, they may ask? Why not join another church? And I confess that if all that I knew of Reverend Wright were the snippets of those sermons that have run in an endless loop on the television and You Tube, or if Trinity United Church of Christ conformed to the caricatures being peddled by some commentators, there is no doubt that I would react in much the same way

But the truth is, that isn't all that I know of the man. The man I met more than twenty years ago is a man who helped introduce me to my Christian faith, a man who spoke to me about our obligations to love one another, to care for the sick, and lift up the poor.

He is a man who served his country as a U.S. Marine, who has studied and lectured at some of the finest universities and seminaries in the country, and who for over thirty years led a church that serves the community by doing God's work here on Earth—by housing the homeless, ministering to the needy, providing day care services and scholarships and prison ministries, and reaching out to those suffering from HIV/AIDS.

In my first book, *Dreams From My Father*, I described the experience of my first service at Trinity:

"People began to shout, to rise from their seats and clap and cry out, a forceful wind carrying the reverend's voice up into the rafters....And in that single note—hope! I heard something else; at the foot of that cross, inside the thousands of churches across the city, I imagined the stories of ordinary black people merging with the stories of David and Goliath, Moses and Pharaoh, the Christians in the lion's den, Ezekiel's field of dry bones.

Those stories—of survival, and freedom, and hope—became our story, my story; the blood that had spilled was our blood, the tears our tears; until this black church, on this bright day, seemed once more a vessel carrying the story of a people into future generations and into a larger world. Our trials and triumphs became at once unique and universal, black and more than black; in chronicling our journey, the stories and songs gave us a means to reclaim memories that we didn't need to feel shame about...memories that all people might study and cherish—and with which we could start to rebuild."

That has been my experience at Trinity. Like other pre-dominantly black churches across the country, Trinity embodies the black community in its entirety—the doctor and the welfare mom, the model student and the former gang-banger. Like other black churches, Trinity's services are full of raucous laughter and sometimes bawdy humor. They are full of dancing, clapping, screaming, and shouting that may seem jarring to the untrained ear.

The church contains in full the kindness and cruelty, the fierce intelligence and the shocking ignorance, the struggles and successes, the love and yes, the bitterness and bias that make up the black experience in America.

And this helps explain, perhaps, my relationship with Reverend Wright. As imperfect as he may be, he has been like family to me. He strengthened my faith, officiated my wedding, and baptized my children. Not once in my conversations with him have I heard him talk about any ethnic group in derogatory terms, or treat whites with whom he interacted with anything but courtesy and respect. He contains within him the contradictions—the good and the bad—of the community that he has served diligently for so many years.

I can no more disown him than I can disown the black community. I can no more disown him than I can my white grandmother—a woman who helped raise me, a woman who sacrificed again and again for me, a woman who loves me as much as she loves anything in this world, but a woman who once confessed her fear of black men who passed by her on the street, and who on more than one occasion has uttered racial or ethnic stereotypes that made me cringe.

These people are a part of me. And they are a part of America, this country that I love.

Some will see this as an attempt to justify or excuse comments that are simply inexcusable. I can assure you it is not. I suppose the politically safe thing would be to move on from this episode and just hope that it fades into the woodwork.

We can dismiss Reverend Wright as a crank or a demagogue, just as some have dismissed Geraldine Ferraro, in the aftermath of her recent statements, as harboring some deep-seated racial bias.

But race is an issue that I believe this nation cannot afford to ignore right now. We would be making the same mistake that Reverend Wright made in his offending sermons about America—to simplify and stereotype and amplify the negative to the point that it distorts reality.

The fact is that the comments that have been made and the issues that have surfaced over the last few weeks reflect the complexities of race in this country that we've never really worked through—a part of our union that we have yet to perfect.

And if we walk away now, if we simply retreat into our respective corners, we will never be able to come together and solve challenges like health care, or education, or the need to find good jobs for every American.

Understanding this reality requires a reminder of how we arrived at this point. As William Faulkner once wrote, "The past isn't dead and buried. In fact, it isn't even past." We do not need to recite here the history of racial injustice in this country. But we do need to remind ourselves that so many of the disparities that exist in the African-American community today can be directly traced to inequalities passed on from an earlier generation that suffered under the brutal legacy of slavery and Jim Crow.

Segregated schools were, and are, inferior schools; we still haven't fixed them, fifty years after Brown v. Board of Education. And the inferior education they provided, then and now, helps explain the pervasive achievement gap between today's black and white students.

Legalized discrimination—where blacks were prevented, often through violence, from owning property, or loans were not granted to African-American business owners, or black home-owners could not access FHA mortgages, or blacks were excluded from unions, or the police force, or fire departments—meant that black families could not amass any meaningful wealth to bequeath to future generations. That history helps explain the wealth and income gap between black and white, and the concentrated pockets of poverty that persists in so many of today's urban and rural communities.

A lack of economic opportunity among black men, and the shame and frustration that came from not being able to provide for one's family, contributed to the erosion of black families—a problem that welfare policies for many years may have worsened. And the lack of basic services in so many urban black neighborhoods—parks for kids to play in, police walking the beat, regular garbage pick-up and building code enforcement—all helped create a cycle of violence, blight, and neglect that continue to haunt us.

This is the reality in which Reverend Wright and other African-Americans of his generation grew up. They came of age in the late fifties and early sixties, a time when segregation was still the law of the land and opportunity was systematically constricted. What's remarkable is not how many failed in the face of discrimination, but rather how many men and women overcame the odds; how many were able to make a way out of no way for those like me who would come after them.

But for all those who scratched and clawed their way to get a piece of the American Dream, there were many who didn't make it—those who were ultimately defeated, in one way or another, by discrimination. That legacy of defeat was passed on to future generations—those young men and increasingly young women who we see standing on street corners or languishing in our prisons, without hope or prospects for the future.

Even for those blacks who did make it, questions of race and racism continue to define their worldview in fundamental ways. For the men and women of Reverend Wright's generation, the memories of humiliation and doubt and fear have not gone away; nor has the anger and the bitterness of those years.

That anger may not get expressed in public, in front of white co-workers or white friends. But it does find voice in the barbershop or around the kitchen table. At times, that anger is exploited by politicians, to gin up votes along racial lines, or to make up for a politician's own failings.

And occasionally it finds voice in the church on Sunday morning, in the pulpit and in the pews. The fact that so many people are surprised to hear that anger in some of Reverend Wright's sermons simply reminds us of the old truism that the most segregated hour in American life occurs on Sunday morning.

That anger is not always productive; indeed, all too often it distracts attention from solving real problems; it keeps us from squarely facing our own complicity in our condition, and prevents the African-American community from forging the alliances it needs to bring about real change.

But the anger is real. It is powerful. And to simply wish it away, to condemn it without understanding its roots, only serves to widen the chasm of misunderstanding that exists between the races.

In fact, a similar anger exists within segments of the white community. Most working and middle-class white Americans don't feel that they have been particularly privileged by their race. Their experience is the immigrant experience. As far as they're concerned, no one's handed them anything. They've built it from scratch. They've worked hard all their lives, many times only to see their jobs shipped overseas or their pension dumped after a lifetime of labor. They are anxious about their futures, and feel their dreams slipping away. In an era of stagnant wages and global competition, opportunity comes to be seen as a zero sum game, in which your dreams come at my expense.

So when they are told to bus their children to a school across town; when they hear that an African American is getting an advantage in landing a good job or a spot in a good college because of an injustice that they themselves never committed; when they're told that their fears about crime in urban neighborhoods are somehow prejudiced, resentment builds over time.

Like the anger within the black community, these resentments aren't always expressed in polite company. But they have helped shape the political landscape for at least a generation. Anger over welfare and affirmative action helped forge the Reagan Coalition. Politicians routinely exploited fears of crime for their own electoral ends.

Talk show hosts and conservative commentators built entire careers unmasking bogus claims of racism while dismissing legitimate discussions of racial injustice and inequality as mere political correctness or reverse racism.

Just as black anger often proved counterproductive, so have these white resentments distracted attention from the real culprits of the middle class squeeze—a corporate culture rife with inside dealing, questionable accounting practices, and short-term greed; a Washington dominated by lobbyists and special interests; economic policies that favor the few over the many.

And yet, to wish away the resentments of white Americans, to label them as misguided or even racist, without recognizing they are grounded in legitimate concerns—this too widens the racial divide and blocks the path to understanding.

This is where we are right now. It's a racial stalemate we've been stuck in for years. Contrary to the claims of some of my critics, black and white, I have never been so naïve as to believe that we can get beyond our racial divisions in a single election cycle, or with a single candidacy—particularly a candidacy as imperfect as my own.

But I have asserted a firm conviction—a conviction rooted in my faith in God and my faith in the American people—that working together we can move beyond some of our old racial wounds, and that in fact we have no choice if we are to continue on the path of a more perfect union.

For the African-American community, that path means embracing the burdens of our past without becoming victims of our past. It means continuing to insist on a full measure of justice in every aspect of American life. But it also means binding our particular grievances—for better health care, and better schools, and better jobs—to the larger aspirations of all Americans—the white woman struggling to break the glass ceiling, the white man whose been laid off, the immigrant trying to feed his family.

And it means taking full responsibility for our own lives—by demanding more from our fathers, and spending more time with our children, and reading to them, and teaching them that while they may face challenges and discrimination in their own lives, they must never succumb to despair or cynicism; they must always believe that they can write their own destiny.

Ironically, this quintessentially American, and yes, conservative notion of self-help found frequent expression in Reverend Wright's sermons. But what my former pastor too often failed to understand is that embarking on a program of self-help also requires a belief that society can change.

The profound mistake of Reverend Wright's sermons is not that he spoke about racism in our society. It's that he spoke as if our society was static; as if no progress has been made; as if this country—a country that has made it possible for one of his own members to run for the highest office in the land and build a coalition of white and black, Latino and Asian, rich and poor, young and old—is still irrevocably bound to a tragic past.

But what we know—what we have seen—is that America can change. That is true genius of this nation. What we have already achieved gives us hope—the audacity to hope for what we can and must achieve tomorrow.

In the white community, the path to a more perfect union means acknowledging that what ails the African-American community does not just exist in the minds of black people; that the legacy of discrimination and current incidents of discrimination, while less overt than in the past are real and must be addressed. Not just with words, but with deeds—by investing in our schools and our communities, by enforcing our civil rights laws and ensuring fairness in our criminal justice system, by providing this generation with ladders of opportunity that were unavailable for previous generations.

It requires all Americans to realize that your dreams do not have to come at the expense of my dreams; that investing in the health, welfare, and education of black and brown and white children will ultimately help all of America prosper.

In the end, then, what is called for is nothing more and nothing less than what all the world's great religions demand—that we do unto others as we would have them do unto us. Let us be our brother's keeper, Scripture tells us. Let us be our sister's keeper. Let us find that common stake we all have in one another, and let our politics reflect that spirit as well.

For we have a choice in this country. We can accept a politics that breeds division, and conflict, and cynicism. We can tackle race only as spectacle—as we did in the OJ trial—or in the wake of tragedy, as we did in the aftermath of Katrina—or as fodder for the nightly news.

We can play Reverend Wright's sermons on every channel, every day and talk about them from now until the election, and make the only question in this campaign whether or not the American people think that I somehow believe or sympathize with his most offensive words.

We can pounce on some gaffe by a Hillary supporter as evidence that she's playing the race card, or we can speculate on whether white men will all flock to John McCain in the general election regardless of his policies.

We can do that.

THE VOICE THAT CHANGED A NATION

But if we do, I can tell you that in the next election, we'll be talking about some other distraction. And then another one. And then another one. And nothing will change.

That is one option, or, at this moment, in this election, we can come together and say: Not this time. This time we want to talk about the crumbling schools that are stealing the future of black children, and white children, and Asian children, and Hispanic children, and Native American children.

This time we want to reject the cynicism that tells us that these kids can't learn; that those kids who don't look like us are somebody else's problem. The children of America are not those kids, they are our kids, and we will not let them fall behind in a 21st century economy. Not this time.

This time we want to talk about how the lines in the emergency room are filled with whites and blacks and Hispanics who do not have health care; who don't have the power on their own to overcome the special interests in Washington, but who can take them on if we do it together.

This time we want to talk about the shuttered mills that once provided a decent life for men and women of every race, and the homes for sale that once belonged to Americans from every religion, every region, every walk of life. This time we want to talk about the fact that the real problem is not that someone who doesn't look like you might take your job—it's that the corporation you work for will ship it overseas for nothing more than a profit.

This time we want to talk about the men and women of every color and creed who serve together, and fight together, and bleed together under the same proud flag. We want to talk about how to bring them home from a war that never should've been authorized and never should've been waged, and we want to talk about how we'll show our patriotism by caring for them, and their families, and giving them the benefits they have earned.

I would not be running for President if I didn't believe with all my heart that this is what the vast majority of Americans want for this country.

This union may never be perfect, but generation after generation has shown that it can always be perfected.

And today, whenever I find myself feeling doubtful or cynical about this possibility, what gives me the most hope is the next generation—the young people whose attitudes and beliefs and openness to change have already made history in this election.

There is one story in particular that I'd like to leave you with today—a story I told when I had the great honor of speaking on Dr. King's birthday at his home church, Ebenezer Baptist, in Atlanta.

There is a young, twenty-three year old white woman named Ashley Baia who organized for our campaign in Florence, South Carolina. She had been working to organize a mostly African-American community since the beginning of this campaign, and one day she was at a roundtable discussion where everyone went around telling their story and why they were there.

And Ashley said that when she was nine years old, her mother got cancer. And because she had to miss days of work, she was let go and lost her health care. They had to file for bankruptcy, and that's when Ashley decided that she had to do something to help her mom.

She knew that food was one of their most expensive costs, and so Ashley convinced her mother that what she really liked and really wanted to eat more than anything else was mustard and relish sandwiches. Because that was the cheapest way to eat.

She did this for a year until her mom got better, and she told everyone at the roundtable that the reason she joined our campaign was so that she could help the millions of other children in the country who want and need to help their parents too.

Now Ashley might have made a different choice. Perhaps somebody told her along the way that the source of her mother's problems were blacks who were on welfare and too lazy to work, or Hispanics who were coming into the country illegally. But she didn't. She sought out allies in her fight against injustice.

Anyway, Ashley finishes her story and then goes around the room and asks everyone else why they're supporting the campaign. They all have different stories and reasons. Many bring up a specific issue. And finally they come to this elderly black man who's been sitting there quietly the entire time. And Ashley asks him why he's there. And he does not bring up a specific issue.

He does not say health care or the economy. He does not say education or the war. He does not say that he was there because of Barack Obama. He simply says to everyone in the room, "I am here because of Ashley."

"I'm here because of Ashley." By itself, that single moment of recognition between that young white girl and that old black man is not enough. It is not enough to give health care to the sick, or jobs to the jobless, or education to our children.

But it is where we start. It is where our union grows stronger. And as so many generations have come to realize over the course of the 221 years since a band of patriots signed that document in Philadelphia, that is where the perfection begins.

Presumptive Nominee Speech

Final Primary Night
St. Paul, Minnesota
June 3, 2008

Tonight, after fifty-four hard fought contests, our primary season has finally come to an end.

Sixteen months have passed since we first stood together on the steps of the Old State Capitol in Springfield, Illinois. Thousands of miles have been traveled. Millions of voices have been heard. And because of what you said—because you decided that change must come to Washington; because you believed that this year must be different than all the rest; because you chose to listen not to your doubts or your fears but to your greatest hopes and highest aspirations, tonight we mark the end of one historic journey with the beginning of another. A journey that will bring a new and better day to America.

Tonight, I can stand before you and say that I will be the Democratic nominee for President of the United States.

I want to thank every American who stood with us over the course of this campaign—through the good days and the bad, from the snows of Cedar Rapids to the sunshine of Sioux Falls. And tonight I also want to thank the men and woman who took this journey with me as fellow candidates for President.

At this defining moment for our nation, we should be proud that our party put forth one of the most talented, qualified field of individuals ever to run for this office. I have not just competed with them as rivals, I have learned from them as friends, as public servants, and as patriots who love America and are willing to work tirelessly to make this country better. They are leaders of this party and leaders that America will turn to for years to come.

That is particularly true for the candidate who has traveled further on this journey than anyone else. Senator Hillary Clinton has made history in this campaign not just because she's a woman who has done what no woman has done before, but because she's a leader who inspires millions of Americans with her strength, her courage, and her commitment to the causes that brought us here tonight.

We've certainly had our differences over the last sixteen months. But as someone who's shared a stage with her many times, I can tell you that what gets Hillary Clinton up in the morning—even in the face of tough odds—is exactly what sent her and Bill Clinton to sign up for their first campaign in Texas all those years ago; what sent her to work at the Children's Defense Fund and made her fight for health care as First Lady; what led her to the United States Senate and fueled her barrier-breaking campaign for the presidency—an unyielding desire to improve the lives of ordinary Americans, no matter how difficult the fight may be.

And you can rest assured that when we finally win the battle for universal health care in this country, she will be central to that victory. When we transform our energy policy and lift our children out of poverty, it will be because she worked to help make it happen. Our party and our country are better off because of her, and I am a better candidate for having had the honor to compete with Hillary Rodham Clinton.

There are those who say that this primary has somehow left us weaker and more divided. Well I say, that because of this primary, there are millions of Americans who have cast their ballot for the very first time. There are Independents and Republicans who understand that this election isn't just about the party in charge of Washington; it's about the need to change Washington.

There are young people, and African-Americans, and Latinos, and women of all ages who have voted in numbers that have broken records and inspired a nation.

All of you chose to support a candidate you believe in deeply. But at the end of the day, we aren't the reason you came out and waited in lines that stretched block after block to make your voice heard. You didn't do that because of me or Senator Clinton or anyone else. You did it because you know in your hearts that at this moment—a moment that will define a generation—we cannot afford to keep doing what we've been doing.

We owe our children a better future. We owe our country a better future. And for all those who dream of that future tonight, I say: let us begin the work together. Let us unite in common effort to chart a new course for America.

In just a few short months, the Republican Party will arrive in St. Paul with a very different agenda. They will come here to nominate John McCain, a man who has served this country heroically. I honor that service and I respect his many accomplishments, even if he chooses to deny mine. My differences with him are not personal; they are with the policies he has proposed in this campaign.

Because while John McCain can legitimately tout moments of independence from his party in the past, such independence has not been the hallmark of his presidential campaign.

It's not change when John McCain decided to stand with George Bush ninety-five percent of the time, as he did in the Senate last year.

It's not change when he offers four more years of Bush economic policies that have failed to create well-paying jobs, or insure our workers, or help Americans afford the skyrocketing cost of college—policies that have lowered the real incomes of the average American family, widened the gap between Wall Street and Main Street, and left our children with a mountain of debt.

And it's not change when he promises to continue a policy in Iraq that asks everything of our brave men and women in uniform and nothing of Iraqi politicians. A policy where all we look for are reasons to stay in Iraq, while we spend billions of dollars a month on a war that isn't making the American people any safer.

So I'll say this: there are many words to describe John McCain's attempt to pass off his embrace of George Bush's policies as bipartisan and new. But change is not one of them.

Change is a foreign policy that doesn't begin and end with a war that should've never been authorized and never been waged. I won't stand here and pretend that there are many good options left in Iraq, but what's not an option is leaving our troops in that country for the next hundred years—

especially at a time when our military is overstretched, our nation is isolated, and nearly every other threat to America is being ignored.

We must be as careful getting out of Iraq as we were careless getting in—but start leaving we must. It's time for Iraqis to take responsibility for their future. It's time to rebuild our military and give our veterans the care they need and the benefits they deserve when they come home. It's time to refocus our efforts on al Qaeda's leadership and Afghanistan, and rally the world against the common threats of the 21st century—terrorism and nuclear weapons, climate change and poverty, genocide and disease. That's what change is.

Change is realizing that meeting today's threats requires not just our firepower, but the power of our diplomacy—tough, direct diplomacy where the President of the United States isn't afraid to let any petty dictator know where America stands and what we stand for.

We must once again have the courage and conviction to lead the free world. That is the legacy of Roosevelt, and Truman, and Kennedy. That's what the American people want. That's what change is.

Change is building an economy that rewards not just wealth, but the work and workers who created it. It's understanding that the struggles facing working families can't be solved by spending billions of dollars on more tax breaks for big corporations and wealthy CEOs, but by giving a the middle-class a tax break, and investing in our crumbling infrastructure, and transforming how we use energy, and improving our schools, and renewing our commitment to science and innovation. It's understanding that fiscal responsibility and shared prosperity can go hand-in-hand, as they did when Bill Clinton was President.

John McCain has spent a lot of time talking about trips to Iraq in the last few weeks, but maybe if he spent some time taking trips to the cities and towns that have been hardest hit by this economy—cities in Michigan, and Ohio, and right here in Minnesota—he'd understand the kind of change that people are looking for.

Maybe if he went to Iowa and met the student who works the night shift after a full day of class and still can't pay the medical bills for a sister who's ill, he'd understand that she can't afford four more years of a health care plan that only takes care of the healthy and wealthy. She needs us to pass health care plan that guarantees insurance to every American who wants it and brings down premiums for every family who needs it. That's the change we need.

Maybe if he went to Pennsylvania and met the man who lost his job but can't even afford the gas to drive around and look for a new one, he'd understand that we can't afford four more years of our addiction to oil from dictators.

That man needs us to pass an energy policy that works with automakers to raise fuel standards, and makes corporations pay for their pollution, and oil companies invest their record profits in a clean energy future—an energy policy that will create millions of new jobs that pay well and can't be outsourced.

That's the change we need.

And maybe if he spent some time in the schools of South Carolina or St. Paul, or where he spoke tonight in New

THE VOICE THAT CHANGED A NATION

Orleans, he'd understand that we can't afford to leave the money behind for No Child Left Behind; that we owe it to our children to invest in early childhood education; to recruit an army of new teachers and give them better pay and more support; to finally decide that in this global economy, the chance to get a college education should not be a privilege for the wealthy few, but the birthright of every American.

That's the change we need in America. That's why I'm running for President.

The other side will come here in September and offer a very different set of policies and positions, and that is a debate I look forward to. It is a debate the American people deserve. But what you don't deserve is another election that's governed by fear, and innuendo, and division. What you won't hear from this campaign or this party is the kind of politics that uses religion as a wedge, and patriotism as a bludgeon—that sees our opponents not as competitors to challenge, but enemies to demonize. Because we may call ourselves Democrats and Republicans, but we are Americans first.

We are always Americans first.

Despite what the good Senator from Arizona said tonight, I have seen people of differing views and opinions find common cause many times during my two decades in public life, and I have brought many together myself.

I've walked arm-in-arm with community leaders on the South Side of Chicago and watched tensions fade as black, white, and Latino fought together for good jobs and good schools. I've sat across the table from law enforcement and civil rights advocates to reform a criminal justice system that sent thirteen innocent people to death row.

And I've worked with friends in the other party to provide more children with health insurance and more working families with a tax break, to curb the spread of nuclear weapons and ensure that the American people know where their tax dollars are being spent, and to reduce the influence of lobbyists who have all too often set the agenda in Washington.

In our country, I have found that this cooperation happens not because we agree on everything, but because behind all the labels and false divisions and categories that define us, beyond all the petty bickering and point-scoring in Washington—Americans are a decent, generous, com-passssionate people, united by common challenges and common hopes. And every so often, there are moments which call on that fundamental goodness to make this country great again.

So it was for that band of patriots who declared in a Philadelphia hall the formation of a more perfect union; and for all those who gave on the fields of Gettysburg and Antietam their last full measure of devotion to save that same union.

So it was for the Greatest Generation that conquered fear itself, and liberated a continent from tyranny, and made this country home to untold opportunity and prosperity.

So it was for the workers who stood out on the picket lines, the women who shattered glass ceilings, the children who braved a Selma bridge for freedom's cause.

So it has been for every generation that faced down the greatest challenges and the most improbable odds to leave their children a world that's better, and kinder, and more just.

And so it must be for us.

America, this is our moment. This is our time. Our time to turn the page on the policies of the past. Our time to bring new energy and new ideas to the challenges we face. Our time to offer a new direction for the country we love.

The journey will be difficult. The road will be long. I face this challenge with profound humility and knowledge of my own limitations. But I also face it with limitless faith in the capacity of the American people.

Because if we are willing to work for it and fight for it, and believe in it, then I am absolutely certain that generations from now, we will be able to look back and tell our children that this was the moment when we began to provide care for the sick and good jobs to the jobless. This was the moment when the rise of the oceans began to slow and our planet began to heal. This was the moment when we ended a war and secured our nation and restored our image as the last, best hope on Earth.

This was the moment—this was the time—when we came together to remake this great nation so that it may always reflect our very best selves and our highest ideals.

Thank you. God Bless you, and may God Bless the United States of America.

A World That Stands as One

Berlin, Germany
July 24, 2008

I come to Berlin as so many of my countrymen have come before. Tonight, I speak to you not as a candidate for President, but as a citizen—a proud citizen of the United States, and a fellow citizen of the world.

I know that I don't look like the Americans who've previously spoken in this great city. The journey that led me here is improbable. My mother was born in the heartland of America, but my father grew up herding goats in Kenya. His father—my grandfather—was a cook, a domestic servant to the British.

At the height of the Cold War, my father decided, like so many others in the forgotten corners of the world, that his yearning—his dream—required the freedom and opportunity promised by the West. And so he wrote letter after letter to universities all across America until somebody, somewhere answered his prayer for a better life.

That is why I'm here. And you are here because you too know that yearning. This city, of all cities, knows the dream of freedom. And you know that the only reason we stand here tonight is because men and women from both of our nations came together to work, and struggle, and sacrifice for that better life.

Ours is a partnership that truly began sixty years ago this summer, on the day when the first American plane touched down at Templehof.

On that day, much of this continent still lay in ruin. The rubble of this city had yet to be built into a wall. The Soviet shadow had swept across Eastern Europe, while in the West, America, Britain, and France took stock of their losses and pondered how the world might be remade.

This is where the two sides met. And on the twenty-fourth of June, 1948, the Communists chose to blockade the western part of the city. They cut off food and supplies to more than two million Germans in an effort to extinguish the last flame of freedom in Berlin.

The size of our forces was no match for the much larger Soviet Army. And yet, retreat would have allowed Communism to march across Europe. Where the last war had ended, another World War could have easily begun. All that stood in the way was Berlin.

And that's when the airlift began—when the largest and most unlikely rescue in history brought food and hope to the people of this city.

The odds were stacked against success. In the winter, a heavy fog filled the sky above, and many planes were forced to turn back without dropping off the needed supplies. The streets where we stand were filled with hungry families who had no comfort from the cold.

But in the darkest hours, the people of Berlin kept the flame of hope burning. The people of Berlin refused to give up. And on one fall day, hundreds of thousands of Berliners came here, to the Tiergarten, and heard the city's mayor implore the world not to give up on freedom. "There is only one possibility," he said, "for us to stand together united until this battle is won...The people of Berlin have spoken. We have done

THE VOICE THAT CHANGED A NATION

our duty, and we will keep on doing our duty. People of the world: now do your duty...People of the world, look at Berlin!" People of the world—look at Berlin!

Look at Berlin, where Germans and Americans learned to work together and trust each other less than three years after facing each other on the field of battle.

Look at Berlin, where the determination of a people met the generosity of the Marshall Plan and created a German miracle; where a victory over tyranny gave rise to NATO, the greatest alliance ever formed to defend our common security.

Look at Berlin, where the bullet holes in the buildings and the somber stones and pillars near the Brandenburg Gate insist that we never forget our common humanity. People of the world—look at Berlin, where a wall came down, a continent came together, and history proved that there is no challenge too great for a world that stands as one.

Sixty years after the airlift, we are called upon again. History has led us to a new crossroad, with new promise and new peril. When you, the German people, tore down that wall—a wall that divided East and West, freedom and tyranny, fear and hope—walls came tumbling down around the world.

From Kiev to Cape Town, prison camps were closed and the doors of democracy were opened. Markets opened too, and the spread of information and technology reduced barriers to opportunity and prosperity. While the 20th century taught us that we share a common destiny, the 21st has revealed a world more intertwined than at any time in human history.

The fall of the Berlin Wall brought new hope. But that very closeness has given rise to new dangers—dangers that cannot be contained within the borders of a country or by the distance of an ocean.

The terrorists of September 11th—plotted in Hamburg and trained in Kandahar and Karachi—before killing thousands from all over the globe on American soil.

As we speak, cars in Boston and factories in Beijing are melting the ice caps in the Arctic, shrinking coastlines in the Atlantic, and bringing drought to farms from Kansas to Kenya.

Poorly secured nuclear material in the former Soviet Union, or secrets from a scientist in Pakistan could help build a bomb that detonates in Paris. The poppies in Afghanistan become the heroin in Berlin. The poverty and violence in Somalia breeds the terror of tomorrow. The genocide in Darfur shames the conscience of us all.

In this new world, such dangerous currents have swept along faster than our efforts to contain them. That is why we cannot afford to be divided. No one nation, no matter how large or powerful, can defeat such challenges alone. None of us can deny these threats, or escape responsibility in meeting them. Yet, in the absence of Soviet tanks and a terrible wall, it has become easy to forget this truth. And if we're honest with each other, we know that sometimes, on both sides of the Atlantic, we have drifted apart and forgotten our shared destiny.

In Europe, the view that America is part of what has gone wrong in our world, rather than a force to help make it right, has become all too common. In America, there are voices that deride and deny the importance of Europe's role in our security and our future.

Both views miss the truth—that Europeans today are bearing new burdens and taking more responsibility in critical parts of the world; and that just as American bases built in the last century still help to defend the security of this continent, so does our country still sacrifice greatly for freedom around the globe.

Yes, there have been differences between America and Europe. No doubt, there will be differences in the future. But the burdens of global citizenship continue to bind us together. A change of leadership in Washington will not lift this burden. In this new century, Americans and Europeans alike will be required to do more—not less. Partnership and cooperation among nations is not a choice; it is the one way, the only way, to protect our common security and advance our common humanity.

That is why the greatest danger of all is to allow new walls to divide us from one another.

The walls between old allies on either side of the Atlantic cannot stand. The walls between the countries with the most and those with the least cannot stand. The walls between races and tribes, natives and immigrants, Christian and Muslim and Jew cannot stand. These now are the walls we must tear down.

We know they have fallen before. After centuries of strife, the people of Europe have formed a Union of promise and prosperity. Here, at the base of a column built to mark victory in war, we meet in the center of a Europe at peace. Not only have walls come down in Berlin, but they have come down in Belfast, where Protestant and Catholic found a way to live together; in the Balkans, where our Atlantic alliance ended wars and brought savage war criminals to justice; and in

South Africa, where the struggle of a courageous people defeated apartheid.

So history reminds us that walls can be torn down. But the task is never easy. True partnership and true progress requires constant work and sustained sacrifice. They require sharing the burdens of development and diplomacy, of progress and peace. They require allies who will listen to each other, learn from each other and, most of all, trust each other.

That is why America cannot turn inward. That is why Europe cannot turn inward. America has no better partner than Europe. Now is the time to build new bridges across the globe as strong as the one that bound us across the Atlantic. Now is the time to join together—through constant cooperation, strong institutions, shared sacrifice, and a global commitment to progress—to meet the challenges of the 21st century.

It was this spirit that led airlift planes to appear in the sky above our heads, and people to assemble where we stand today. And this is the moment when our nations, and all nations, must summon that spirit anew.

This is the moment when we must defeat terror and dry up the well of extremism that supports it. This threat is real and we cannot shrink from our responsibility to combat it. If we could create NATO to face down the Soviet Union, we can join in a new and global partnership to dismantle the networks that have struck in Madrid and Amman, in London and Bali, in Washington and New York.

If we could win a battle of ideas against the communists, we can stand with the vast majority of Muslims who reject the extremism that leads to hate instead of hope.

This is the moment when we must renew our resolve to rout the terrorists who threaten our security in Afghanistan, and the traffickers who sell drugs on your streets. No one welcomes war. I recognize the enormous difficulties in Afghanistan. But my country and yours have a stake in seeing that NATO's first mission beyond Europe's borders is a success.

For the people of Afghanistan, and for our shared security, the work must be done. America cannot do this alone. The Afghan people need our troops and your troops; our support and your support to defeat the Taliban and al Qaeda, to develop their economy, and to help them rebuild their nation. We have too much at stake to turn back now.

This is the moment when we must renew the goal of a world without nuclear weapons. The two superpowers that faced each other across the wall of this city came too close too often to destroying all we have built and all that we love. With that wall gone, we need not stand idly by and watch the further spread of the deadly atom. It is time to secure all loose nuclear materials, to stop the spread of nuclear weapons, and to reduce the arsenals from another era. This is the moment to begin the work of seeking the peace of a world without nuclear weapons.

This is the moment when every nation in Europe must have the chance to choose its own tomorrow free from the shadows of yesterday. In this century, we need a strong European Union that deepens the security and prosperity of this continent, while extending a hand abroad. In this century—in this city of all cities—we must reject the Cold War mind-set of the past, and resolve to work with Russia when we can, to stand up for our values when we must, and to seek a partnership that extends across this entire continent.

This is the moment when we must build on the wealth that open markets have created, and share its benefits more equitably. Trade has been a cornerstone of our growth and global development. But we will not be able to sustain this growth if it favors the few, and not the many. Together, we must forge trade that truly rewards the work that creates wealth, with meaningful protections for our people and our planet. This is the moment for trade that is free and fair for all.

This is the moment we must help answer the call for a new dawn in the Middle East. My country must stand with yours and with Europe in sending a direct message to Iran that it must abandon its nuclear ambitions. We must support the Lebanese who have marched and bled for democracy, and the Israelis and Palestinians who seek a secure and lasting peace.

And despite past differences, this is the moment when the world should support the millions of Iraqis who seek to rebuild their lives, even as we pass responsibility to the Iraqi government and finally bring this war to a close.

This is the moment when we must come together to save this planet. Let us resolve that we will not leave our children a world where the oceans rise, and famine spreads, and terrible storms devastate our lands. Let us resolve that all nations—including my own—will act with the same seriousness of purpose as has your nation, and reduce the carbon we send into our atmosphere. This is the moment to give our children back their future. This is the moment to stand as one.

And this is the moment when we must give hope to those left behind in a globalized world. We must remember that the Cold War born in this city was not a battle for land or treasure. Sixty years ago, the planes that flew over Berlin did not drop bombs; instead they delivered food, and coal, and candy to grateful children. And in that show of solidarity, those pilots won more than a military victory. They won hearts and minds, love and loyalty, and trust—not just from the people in this city, but from all those who heard the story of what they did here.

Now the world will watch and remember what we do here— what we do with this moment. Will we extend our hand to the people in the forgotten corners of this world who yearn for lives marked by dignity and opportunity, by security and justice? Will we lift the child in Bangladesh from poverty, shelter the refugee in Chad, and banish the scourge of AIDS in our time?

Will we stand for the human rights of the dissident in Burma, the blogger in Iran, or the voter in Zimbabwe? Will we give meaning to the words "never again" in Darfur?

Will we acknowledge that there is no more powerful example than the one each of our nations projects to the world? Will we reject torture and stand for the rule of law? Will we welcome immigrants from different lands, and shun discrimination against those who don't look like us or worship like we do, and keep the promise of equality and opportunity for all of our people?

People of Berlin—people of the world—this is our moment. This is our time.

I know my country has not perfected itself. At times, we've struggled to keep the promise of liberty and equality for all of our people. We've made our share of mistakes, and there are times when our actions around the world have not lived up to our best intentions.

But I also know how much I love America. I know that for more than two centuries, we have strived—at great cost and great sacrifice—to form a more perfect union, to seek with other nations a more hopeful world. Our allegiance has never been to any particular tribe or kingdom. Indeed, every language is spoken in our country, every culture has left its imprint on ours, every point of view is expressed in our public squares.

What has always united us—what has always driven our people, what drew my father to America's shores—is a set of ideals that speak to aspirations shared by all people: that we can live free from fear and free from want, that we can speak our minds and assemble with whomever we choose and worship as we please.

Those are the aspirations that joined the fates of all nations in this city. Those aspirations are bigger than anything that drives us apart. It is because of those aspirations that the airlift began. It is because of those aspirations that all free people, everywhere, became citizens of Berlin. It is in pursuit of those aspirations that a new generation—our generation—must make our mark on history.

People of Berlin—and people of the world—the scale of our challenge is great. The road ahead will be long. But I come before you to say that we are heirs to a struggle for freedom. We are a people of improbable hope. Let us build on our common history and seize our common destiny, and once again engage in that noble struggle to bring justice and peace to our world.

The American Promise

Acceptance Speech at the Democratic Convention
Mile High Stadium, Denver Colorado
August 28, 2008

With profound gratitude and great humility, I accept your nomination for the presidency of the United States.

Let me express my thanks to the historic slate of candidates who accompanied me on this journey, and especially the one who traveled the farthest—a champion for working Americans and an inspiration to my daughters and to yours—Hillary Rodham Clinton. To President Clinton, who last night made the case for change as only he can make it; to Ted Kennedy, who embodies the spirit of service; and to the next Vice President of the United States, Joe Biden, I thank you. I am grateful to finish this journey with one of the finest statesmen of our time, a man at ease with everyone from world leaders to the conductors on the Amtrak train he still takes home every night.

To the love of my life, our next First Lady, Michelle Obama, and to Sasha and Malia—I love you so much, and I'm so proud of all of you.

Four years ago, I stood before you and told you my story—of the brief union between a young man from Kenya and a young woman from Kansas who weren't well-off or well-known, but shared a belief that in America, their son could achieve whatever he put his mind to.

It is that promise that has always set this country apart—that through hard work and sacrifice, each of us can pursue our individual dreams but still come together as one American family, to ensure that the next generation can pursue their dreams as well.

That's why I stand here tonight. Because for 232 years, at each moment when that promise was in jeopardy, ordinary men and women, students and soldiers, farmers and teachers, nurses and janitors found the courage to keep it alive.

We meet at one of those defining moments—a moment when our nation is at war, our economy is in turmoil, and the American promise has been threatened once more.

Tonight, more Americans are out of work and more are working harder for less. More of you have lost your homes and even more are watching your home values plummet. More of you have cars you can't afford to drive, credit card bills you can't afford to pay, and tuition that's beyond your reach.

These challenges are not all of government's making. But the failure to respond is a direct result of a broken politics in Washington and the failed policies of George W. Bush.

America, we are better than these last eight years. We are a better country than this.

This country is more decent than one where a woman in Ohio, on the brink of retirement, finds herself one illness away from disaster after a lifetime of hard work.

This country is more generous than one where a man in Indiana has to pack up the equipment he's worked on for twenty years and watch it shipped off to China, and then chokes up as he explains how he felt like a failure when he went home to tell his family the news.

We are more compassionate than a government that lets veterans sleep on our streets and families slide into poverty; that sits on its hands while a major American city drowns before our eyes.

Tonight, I say to the American people, to Democrats and Republicans and Independents across this great land— enough. This moment, this election, is our chance to keep, in the 21st century, the American promise alive. Because next week, in Minnesota, the same party that brought you two terms of George Bush and Dick Cheney will ask this country for a third. And we are here because we love this country too much to let the next four years look like the last eight. On November 4th, we must stand up and say: "Eight is enough."

Now let there be no doubt. The Republican nominee, John McCain, has worn the uniform of our country with bravery and distinction, and for that we owe him our gratitude and respect. And next week, we'll also hear about those occasions when he's broken with his party as evidence that he can deliver the change that we need.

But the record's clear: John McCain has voted with George Bush ninety percent of the time. Senator McCain likes to talk about judgment, but really, what does it say about your judgment when you think George Bush has been right more than ninety percent of the time? I don't know about you, but I'm not ready to take a ten percent chance on change.

The truth is, on issue after issue that would make a difference in your lives—on health care, and education, and the economy—Senator McCain has been anything but independent. He said that our economy has made "great progress" under this President. He said that the fundamentals of the economy are strong. And when one of his chief advisors—the man who wrote his economic plan—was talking about the anxiety Americans are feeling, he said that we were just suffering from a "mental recession," and that we've become, and I quote, "a nation of whiners."

A nation of whiners? Tell that to the proud auto workers at a Michigan plant who, after they found out it was closing, kept showing up every day and working as hard as ever, because they knew there were people who counted on the brakes that they made. Tell that to the military families who shoulder their burdens silently as they watch their loved ones leave for their third or fourth or fifth tour of duty. These are not whiners. They work hard and give back and keep going without complaint. These are the Americans that I know.

Now, I don't believe that Senator McCain doesn't care what's going on in the lives of Americans. I just think he doesn't know. Why else would he define middle-class as someone making under five million dollars a year? How else could he propose hundreds of billions in tax breaks for big corporations and oil companies but not one penny of tax relief to more than one hundred million Americans? How else could he offer a health care plan that would actually tax people's benefits, or an education plan that would do nothing to help families pay for college, or a plan that would privatize Social Security and gamble your retirement?

It's not because John McCain doesn't care. It's because John McCain doesn't get it.

For over two decades, he's subscribed to that old, discredited Republican philosophy: give more and more to those with the most and hope that prosperity trickles down to everyone else. In Washington, they call this the Ownership Society, but what it really means is—you're on your own. Out of work? Tough luck. No health care? The market will fix it. Born into poverty? Pull yourself up by your own bootstraps—even if you don't have boots. You're on your own.

Well it's time for them to own their failure. It's time for us to change America.

You see, we Democrats have a very different measure of what constitutes progress in this country.

We measure progress by how many people can find a job that pays the mortgage; whether you can put a little extra money away at the end of each month so you can someday watch your child receive her college diploma. We measure progress in the 23 million new jobs that were created when Bill Clinton was President—when the average American family saw its income go up $7,500 instead of down $2,000 like it has under George Bush.

We measure the strength of our economy not by the number of billionaires we have or the profits of the Fortune 500, but by whether someone with a good idea can take a risk and start a new business, or whether the waitress who lives on tips can take a day off to look after a sick kid without losing her job— an economy that honors the dignity of work.

The fundamentals we use to measure economic strength are whether we are living up to that fundamental promise that has made this country great—a promise that is the only reason I am standing here tonight.

Because in the faces of those young veterans who come back from Iraq and Afghanistan, I see my grandfather, who signed up after Pearl Harbor, marched in Patton's Army, and was rewarded by a grateful nation with the chance to go to college on the GI Bill.

In the face of that young student, who sleeps just three hours before working the night shift, I think about my mom, who raised my sister and me on her own while she worked and earned her degree; who once turned to food stamps but was still able to send us to the best schools in the country with the help of student loans and scholarships.

When I listen to another worker tell me that his factory has shut down, I remember all those men and women on the South Side of Chicago who I stood by and fought for two decades ago after the local steel plant closed.

And when I hear a woman talk about the difficulties of starting her own business, I think about my grandmother, who worked her way up from the secretarial pool to middle-management, despite years of being passed over for promotions because she was a woman. She's the one who taught me about hard work. She's the one who put off buying a new car or a new dress for herself so that I could have a better life. She poured everything she had into me. And although she can no longer travel, I know that she's watching tonight, and that tonight is her night as well.

I don't know what kind of lives John McCain thinks that celebrities lead, but this has been mine. These are my heroes. Theirs are the stories that shaped me. And it is on their behalf that I intend to win this election and keep our promise alive as President of the United States.

What is that promise?

It's a promise that says each of us has the freedom to make of our own lives what we will, but that we also have the obligation to treat each other with dignity and respect.

It's a promise that says the market should reward drive, and innovation, and generate growth, but that businesses should live up to their responsibilities to create American jobs, look out for American workers, and play by the rules of the road.

Ours is a promise that says government cannot solve all our problems, but what it should do is that which we cannot do for ourselves—protect us from harm and provide every child a decent education, keep our water clean and our toys safe, invest in new schools and new roads and new science and technology.

Our government should work for us, not against us. It should help us, not hurt us. It should ensure opportunity not just for those with the most money and influence, but for every American who's willing to work.

That's the promise of America—the idea that we are responsible for ourselves, but that we also rise or fall as one nation; the fundamental belief that I am my brother's keeper, I am my sister's keeper.

That's the promise we need to keep. That's the change we need right now. So let me spell out exactly what that change would mean if I am President.

Change means a tax code that doesn't reward the lobbyists who wrote it, but the American workers and small businesses who deserve it.

Unlike John McCain, I will stop giving tax breaks to corporations that ship jobs overseas, and I will start giving them to companies that create good jobs right here in America.

I will eliminate capital gains taxes for the small businesses and the start-ups that will create the high-wage, high-tech jobs of tomorrow.

I will cut taxes—cut taxes—for 95% of all working families. Because in an economy like this, the last thing we should do is raise taxes on the middle-class.

And for the sake of our economy, our security, and the future of our planet, I will set a clear goal as President: in ten years, we will finally end our dependence on oil from the Middle East.

Washington's been talking about our oil addiction for the last thirty years, and John McCain has been there for twenty-six of them. In that time, he said no to higher fuel-efficiency standards for cars, no to investments in renewable energy, no to renewable fuels. And today, we import triple the amount of oil as the day that Senator McCain took office.

Now is the time to end this addiction and to understand that drilling is a stop-gap measure, not a long-term solution. Not even close.

As President, I will tap our natural gas reserves, invest in clean coal technology, and find ways to safely harness nuclear power. I'll help our auto companies re-tool, so that the fuel-efficient cars of the future are built right here in America. I'll make it easier for the American people to afford these new cars. And I'll invest 150 billion dollars over the next decade in

THE VOICE THAT CHANGED A NATION

affordable, renewable sources of energy—wind power and solar power and the next generation of bio-fuels; an investment that will lead to new industries and five million new jobs that pay well and can't ever be outsourced.

America, now is not the time for small plans.

Now is the time to finally meet our moral obligation to provide every child a world-class education, because it will take nothing less to compete in the global economy. Michelle and I are only here tonight because we were given a chance at an education. And I will not settle for an America where some kids don't have that chance. I'll invest in early childhood education. I'll recruit an army of new teachers and pay them higher salaries and give them more support. And in exchange, I'll ask for higher standards and more accountability. And we will keep our promise to every young American—if you commit to serving your community or your country, we will make sure you can afford a college education.

Now is the time to finally keep the promise of affordable, accessible health care for every single American. If you have health care, my plan will lower your premiums. If you don't, you'll be able to get the same kind of coverage that members of Congress give themselves. And as someone who watched my mother argue with insurance companies while she lay in bed dying of cancer, I will make certain those companies stop discriminating against those who are sick and need care the most.

Now is the time to help families with paid sick days and better family leave, because nobody in America should have to choose between keeping their jobs and caring for a sick child or ailing parent.

Now is the time to change our bankruptcy laws, so that your pensions are protected ahead of CEO bonuses; and the time to protect Social Security for future generations.

And now is the time to keep the promise of equal pay for an equal day's work, because I want my daughters to have exactly the same opportunities as your sons.

Now many of these plans will cost money, which is why I've laid out how I'll pay for every dime—by closing corporate loopholes and tax havens that don't help America grow. But I will also go through the federal budget, line by line, eliminating programs that no longer work and making the ones we do need work better and cost less—because we cannot meet twenty-first century challenges with a twentieth century bureaucracy.

And Democrats, we must also admit that fulfilling America's promise will require more than just money. It will require a renewed sense of responsibility from each of us to recover what John F. Kennedy called our "intellectual and moral strength."

Yes, government must lead on energy independence, but each of us must do our part to make our homes and businesses more efficient. Yes, we must provide more ladders to success for young men who fall into lives of crime and despair. But we must also admit that programs alone can't replace parents, that government can't turn off the television and make a child do her homework, that fathers must take more responsibility for providing the love and guidance their children need.

Individual responsibility and mutual responsibility—that's the essence of America's promise.

And just as we keep our promise to the next generation here at home, so must we keep America's promise abroad. If John McCain wants to have a debate about who has the temperament and judgment to serve as the next Commander in Chief, that's a debate I'm ready to have.

For while Senator McCain was turning his sights to Iraq just days after 9/11, I stood up and opposed this war, knowing that it would distract us from the real threats we face. When John McCain said we could just "muddle through" in Afghanistan, I argued for more resources and more troops to finish the fight against the terrorists who actually attacked us on 9/11, and made clear that we must take out Osama bin Laden and his lieutenants if we have them in our sights. John McCain likes to say that he'll follow bin Laden to the Gates of Hell—but he won't even go to the cave where he lives.

And today, as my call for a time frame to remove our troops from Iraq has been echoed by the Iraqi government and even the Bush Administration, even after we learned that Iraq has a $79 billion surplus while we're wallowing in deficits, John McCain stands alone in his stubborn refusal to end a misguided war.

That's not the judgment we need. That won't keep America safe. We need a President who can face the threats of the future, not keep grasping at the ideas of the past.

You don't defeat a terrorist network that operates in eighty countries by occupying Iraq. You don't protect Israel and deter Iran just by talking tough in Washington. You can't truly stand up for Georgia when you've strained our oldest alliances. If John McCain wants to follow George Bush with more tough talk and bad strategy, that is his choice—but it is not the change we need.

We are the party of Roosevelt. We are the party of Kennedy. So don't tell me that Democrats won't defend this country. Don't tell me that Democrats won't keep us safe. The Bush-McCain foreign policy has squandered the legacy that generations of Americans—Democrats and Republicans—have built, and we are here to restore that legacy.

As Commander in Chief, I will never hesitate to defend this nation, but I will only send our troops into harm's way with a clear mission and a sacred commitment to give them the equipment they need in battle and the care and benefits they deserve when they come home.

I will end this war in Iraq responsibly, and finish the fight against al Qaeda and the Taliban in Afghanistan. I will rebuild our military to meet future conflicts. But I will also renew the tough, direct diplomacy that can prevent Iran from obtaining nuclear weapons and curb Russian aggression. I will build new partnerships to defeat the threats of the 21st century: terrorism and nuclear proliferation, poverty and genocide, climate change and disease. And I will restore our moral standing, so that America is once again that last, best hope for all who are called to the cause of freedom, who long for lives of peace and who yearn for a better future.

These are the policies I will pursue. And in the weeks ahead, I look forward to debating them with John McCain.

But what I will not do is suggest that the Senator takes his positions for political purposes. Because one of the things that we have to change in our politics is the idea that people cannot disagree without challenging each other's character and patriotism.

The times are too serious, the stakes are too high for this same partisan playbook. So let us agree that patriotism has no party. I love this country and so do you, and so does John McCain. The men and women who serve in our battlefields may be Democrats and Republicans and Independents, but they have fought together and bled together and some died together under the same proud flag. They have not served a red America or a blue America—they have served the United States of America.

So I've got news for you, John McCain: We *all* put our country first.

America, our work will not be easy. The challenges we face require tough choices, and Democrats as well as Republicans will need to cast off the worn-out ideas and politics of the past. For part of what has been lost these past eight years can't just be measured by lost wages or bigger trade deficits. What has also been lost is our sense of common purpose—our sense of higher purpose. And that's what we have to restore.

We may not agree on abortion, but surely we can agree on reducing the number of unwanted pregnancies in this country. The reality of gun ownership may be different for hunters in rural Ohio than for those plagued by gang-violence in Cleveland, but don't tell me we can't uphold the Second Amendment while keeping AK-47s out of the hands of criminals.

I know there are differences on same-sex marriage, but surely we can agree that our gay and lesbian brothers and sisters deserve to visit the person they love in the hospital and to live lives free of discrimination. Passions fly on immigration, but I don't know anyone who benefits when a mother is separated from her infant child or an employer undercuts American wages by hiring illegal workers.

This too is part of America's promise—the promise of a democracy where we can find the strength and grace to bridge divides and unite in common effort.

I know there are those who dismiss such beliefs as happy talk. They claim that our insistence on something larger, something firmer and more honest in our public life is just a Trojan Horse for higher taxes and the abandonment of traditional values. And that's to be expected. Because if you don't have any fresh ideas, then you use stale tactics to scare the voters. If you don't have a record to run on, then you paint your opponent as someone people should run from.

You make a big election about small things.

And you know what—it's worked before. Because it feeds into the cynicism we all have about government. When Washington doesn't work, all its promises seem empty. If your hopes have been dashed again and again, then it's best to stop hoping and settle for what you already know.

I get it. I realize that I am not the likeliest candidate for this office. I don't fit the typical pedigree, and I haven't spent my career in the halls of Washington.

But I stand before you tonight because all across America something is stirring. What the nay-sayers don't understand is that this election has never been about me. It's been about you.

For eighteen long months, you have stood up, one by one, and said enough to the politics of the past. You understand that in this election, the greatest risk we can take is to try the same old politics with the same old players and expect a different result. You have shown what history teaches us—that at defining moments like this one, the change we need doesn't come from Washington. Change comes *to* Washington. Change happens because the American people demand it—because they rise up and insist on new ideas and new leadership, a new politics for a new time.

America, this is one of those moments.

I believe that as hard as it will be, the change we need is coming. Because I've seen it. Because I've lived it. I've seen it in Illinois, when we provided health care to more children and moved more families from welfare to work. I've seen it in Washington, when we worked across party lines to open up government and hold lobbyists more accountable, to give better care for our veterans and keep nuclear weapons out of terrorist hands.

And I've seen it in this campaign, in the young people who voted for the first time, and in those who got involved again after a very long time, in the Republicans who never thought they'd pick up a Democratic ballot, but did. I've seen it in the workers who would rather cut their hours back a day than see their friends lose their jobs, in the soldiers who re-enlist after losing a limb, in the good neighbors who take a stranger in when a hurricane strikes and the floodwaters rise.

This country of ours has more wealth than any nation, but that's not what makes us rich. We have the most powerful military on Earth, but that's not what makes us strong. Our universities and our culture are the envy of the world, but that's not what keeps the world coming to our shores.

Instead, it is that American spirit—that American promise—that pushes us forward, even when the path is uncertain, that binds us together in spite of our differences; that makes us fix our eye not on what is seen, but what is unseen, that better place around the bend.

That promise is our greatest inheritance. It's a promise I make to my daughters when I tuck them in at night, and a promise that you make to yours—a promise that has led immigrants to cross oceans and pioneers to travel west, a promise that led workers to picket lines, and women to reach for the ballot.

And it is that promise that forty five years ago today, brought Americans from every corner of this land to stand together on a Mall in Washington, before Lincoln's Memorial, and hear a young preacher from Georgia speak of his dream.

The men and women who gathered there could've heard many things. They could've heard words of anger and discord. They could've been told to succumb to the fear and frustration of so many dreams deferred.

But what the people heard instead—people of every creed and color, from every walk of life—is that in America, our destiny is inextricably linked. That together, our dreams can be one.

"We cannot walk alone," the preacher cried. "And as we walk, we must make the pledge that we shall always march ahead. We cannot turn back."

America, we cannot turn back. Not with so much work to be done. Not with so many children to educate, and so many veterans to care for. Not with an economy to fix and cities to rebuild and farms to save. Not with so many families to protect and so many lives to mend. America, we cannot turn back. We cannot walk alone.

At this moment, in this election, we must pledge once more to march into the future. Let us keep that promise—that American promise—and in the words of Scripture, hold firmly without wavering, to the hope that we confess.

Thank you, and God Bless the United States of America.

Election Night Victory Speech

Grant Park in Chicago, Illinois
November 4, 2008

If there is anyone out there who still doubts that America is a place where all things are possible, who still wonders if the dream of our founders is alive in our time, who still questions the power of our democracy—tonight is your answer.

It's the answer told by lines that stretched around schools and churches in numbers this nation has never seen; by people who waited three hours and four hours, many for the very first time in their lives, because they believed that this time must be different—that their voice could be that difference.

It's the answer spoken by young and old, rich and poor, Democrat and Republican, black, white, Latino, Asian, Native American, gay, straight, disabled, and not disabled—Americans who sent a message to the world that we have never been a collection of red states and blue states: we are, and always will be, the United States of America.

It's the answer that led those who have been told for so long by so many to be cynical, and fearful, and doubtful of what we can achieve to put their hands on the arc of history and bend it once more toward the hope of a better day.

It's been a long time coming, but tonight, because of what we did on this day, in this election, at this defining moment, change has come to America.

I just received a very gracious call from Senator McCain. He fought long and hard in this campaign, and he's fought even longer and harder for the country he loves. He has endured sacrifices for America that most of us cannot begin to imagine, and we are better off for the service rendered by this brave and selfless leader. I congratulate him and Governor Palin for all they have achieved, and I look forward to working with them to renew this nation's promise in the months ahead.

I want to thank my partner in this journey, a man who campaigned from his heart and spoke for the men and women he grew up with on the streets of Scranton and rode with on that train home to Delaware, the Vice President-elect of the United States, Joe Biden.

I would not be standing here tonight without the unyielding support of my best friend for the last sixteen years, the rock of our family and the love of my life—our nation's next First Lady, Michelle Obama. Sasha and Malia, I love you both so much, and you have earned the new puppy that's coming with us to the White House. And while she's no longer with us, I know my grandmother is watching, along with the family that made me who I am. I miss them tonight, and know that my debt to them is beyond measure.

To my campaign manager David Plouffe, my chief strategist David Axelrod, and the best campaign team ever assembled in the history of politics—you made this happen, and I am forever grateful for what you've sacrificed to get it done.

But above all, I will never forget who this victory truly belongs to—it belongs to you.

I was never the likeliest candidate for this office. We didn't start with much money or many endorsements. Our campaign was not hatched in the halls of Washington. It began in the backyards of Des Moines and the living rooms of Concord and the front porches of Charleston.

It was built by working men and women who dug into what little savings they had to give five dollars and ten dollars and twenty dollars to this cause.

It grew strength from the young people who rejected the myth of their generation's apathy, who left their homes and their families for jobs that offered little pay and less sleep. From the not-so-young people who braved the bitter cold and scorching heat to knock on the doors of perfect strangers, from the millions of Americans who volunteered, and organized, and proved that more than two centuries later, a government of the people, by the people, and for the people has not perished from this Earth.

This is your victory.

I know you didn't do this just to win an election and I know you didn't do it for me. You did it because you understand the enormity of the task that lies ahead. For even as we celebrate tonight, we know the challenges that tomorrow will bring are the greatest of our lifetime—two wars, a planet in peril, the worst financial crisis in a century.

Even as we stand here tonight, we know there are brave Americans waking up in the deserts of Iraq and the mountains of Afghanistan to risk their lives for us. There are mothers and fathers who will lie awake after their children fall asleep and wonder how they'll make the mortgage, or pay their doctor's bills, or save enough for college. There is new energy to harness and new jobs to be created, new schools to build and threats to meet, and alliances to repair.

The road ahead will be long. Our climb will be steep. We may not get there in one year or even one term, but America—I have never been more hopeful than I am tonight that we will get there. I promise you—we as a people will get there.

There will be setbacks and false starts. There are many who won't agree with every decision or policy I make as President, and we know that government can't solve every problem. But I will always be honest with you about the challenges we face. I will listen to you, especially when we disagree. And above all, I will ask you join in the work of remaking this nation the only way it's been done in America for 221 years—block by block, brick by brick, calloused hand by calloused hand.

What began twenty-one months ago in the depths of winter must not end on this autumn night. This victory alone is not the change we seek—it is only the chance for us to make that change. And that cannot happen if we go back to the way things were. It cannot happen without you.

So let us summon a new spirit of patriotism; of service and responsibility where each of us resolves to pitch in and work harder and look after not only ourselves, but each other. Let us remember that if this financial crisis taught us anything, it's that we cannot have a thriving Wall Street while Main Street suffers. In this country, we rise or fall as one nation, as one people.

Let us resist the temptation to fall back on the same partisanship and pettiness and immaturity that has poisoned our politics for so long. Let us remember that it was a man from this state who first carried the banner of the Republican

THE VOICE THAT CHANGED A NATION

Party to the White House—a party founded on the values of self-reliance, individual liberty, and national unity.

Those are values we all share.

And while the Democratic Party has won a great victory tonight, we do so with a measure of humility and determination to heal the divides that have held back our progress. As Lincoln said to a nation far more divided than ours, "We are not enemies, but friends…though passion may have strained, it must not break our bonds of affection."

And to those Americans whose support I have yet to earn—I may not have won your vote, but I hear your voices, I need your help, and I will be your President too.

And to all those watching tonight from beyond our shores, from parliaments and palaces to those who are huddled around radios in the forgotten corners of our world—our stories are singular, but our destiny is shared, and a new dawn of American leadership is at hand.

To those who would tear this world down—we will defeat you. To those who seek peace and security—we support you. And to all those who have wondered if America's beacon still burns as bright—tonight we proved once more that the true strength of our nation comes not from our the might of our arms or the scale of our wealth, but from the enduring power of our ideals: democracy, liberty, opportunity, and unyielding hope.

For that is the true genius of America—that America can change. Our union can be perfected. And what we have already achieved gives us hope for what we can and must achieve tomorrow.

This election had many firsts and many stories that will be told for generations. But one that's on my mind tonight is about a woman who cast her ballot in Atlanta. She's a lot like the millions of others who stood in line to make their voice heard in this election except for one thing - Ann Nixon Cooper is 106 years old.

She was born just a generation past slavery; a time when there were no cars on the road or planes in the sky; when someone like her couldn't vote for two reasons—because she was a woman and because of the color of her skin.

And tonight, I think about all that she's seen throughout her century in America—the heartache and the hope, the struggle and the progress, the times we were told that we can't, and the people who pressed on with that American creed: Yes we can.

At a time when women's voices were silenced and their hopes dismissed, she lived to see them stand up and speak out and reach for the ballot. Yes we can.

When there was despair in the dust bowl and depression across the land, she saw a nation conquer fear itself with a New Deal, new jobs and a new sense of common purpose. Yes we can.

When the bombs fell on our harbor and tyranny threatened the world, she was there to witness a generation rise to greatness and a democracy was saved. Yes we can.

She was there for the buses in Montgomery, the hoses in Birmingham, a bridge in Selma, and a preacher from Atlanta who told a people that, "We Shall Overcome." Yes we can.

A man touched down on the moon, a wall came down in Berlin, a world was connected by our own science and imagination. And this year, in this election, she touched her finger to a screen, and cast her vote, because after 106 years in America, through the best of times and the darkest of hours, she knows how America can change. Yes we can.

America, we have come so far. We have seen so much. But there is so much more to do. So tonight, let us ask ourselves— if our children should live to see the next century, if my daughters should be so lucky to live as long as Ann Nixon Cooper, what change will they see? What progress will we have made?

This is our chance to answer that call.

This is our moment.

This is our time—to put our people back to work and open doors of opportunity for our kids, to restore prosperity and promote the cause of peace, to reclaim the American Dream and reaffirm that fundamental truth—that out of many we are one, that while we breathe we hope, and where we are met with cynicism and doubt, and those who tell us that we can't, we will respond with that timeless creed that sums up the spirit of a people:

Yes We Can.

Thank you, God bless you, and may God Bless the United States of America.

Inaugural Address

National Mall, Washington D.C.
January 20, 2009

"Thank you. Thank you.

My fellow citizens:

I stand here today humbled by the task before us, grateful for the trust you have bestowed, mindful of the sacrifices borne by our ancestors. I thank President Bush for his service to our nation, as well as the generosity and cooperation he has shown throughout this transition.

Forty-four Americans have now taken the presidential oath. The words have been spoken during rising tides of prosperity and the still waters of peace. Yet, every so often, the oath is taken amidst gathering clouds and raging storms. At these moments, America has carried on not simply because of the skill or vision of those in high office, but because We the People have remained faithful to the ideals of our fore bearers and true to our founding documents.

So it has been. So it must be with this generation of Americans.

That we are in the midst of crisis is now well understood. Our nation is at war against a far-reaching network of violence and hatred. Our economy is badly weakened, a consequence of greed and irresponsibility on the part of some, but also our collective failure to make hard choices and prepare the nation for a new age. Homes have been lost; jobs shed; businesses shuttered. Our health care is too costly; our schools fail too many; and each day brings further evidence that the ways we use energy strengthen our adversaries and threaten our planet.

These are the indicators of crisis, subject to data and statistics. Less measurable but no less profound is a sapping of confidence across our land, a nagging fear that America's decline is inevitable, that the next generation must lower its sights.

Today I say to you that the challenges we face are real. They are serious and they are many. They will not be met easily or in a short span of time. But know this, America: They *will* be met.

On this day, we gather because we have chosen hope over fear, unity of purpose over conflict and discord. On this day, we come to proclaim an end to the petty grievances and false promises, the recriminations and worn-out dogmas, that for far too long have strangled our politics.

We remain a young nation, but in the words of Scripture, the time has come to set aside childish things. The time has come to reaffirm our enduring spirit, to choose our better history, to carry forward that precious gift, that noble idea, passed on from generation to generation: the God-given promise that all are equal, all are free, and all deserve a chance to pursue their full measure of happiness.

In reaffirming the greatness of our nation, we understand that greatness is never a given. It must be earned. Our journey has never been one of shortcuts or settling for less. It has not been the path for the fainthearted—for those who prefer leisure over work, or seek only the pleasures of riches and fame.

Rather, it has been the risk-takers, the doers, the makers of things—some celebrated but more often, men and women obscure in their labor—who have carried us up the long, rugged path toward prosperity and freedom.

For us, they packed up their few worldly possessions and traveled across oceans in search of a new life.

For us, they toiled in sweatshops and settled the West, endured the lash of the whip and plowed the hard earth.

For us, they fought and died, in places like Concord and Gettysburg, Normandy and Khe Sahn.

Time and again, these men and women struggled and sacrificed and worked till their hands were raw so that we might live a better life. They saw America as bigger than the sum of our individual ambitions, greater than all the differences of birth or wealth or faction.

This is the journey we continue today.

We remain the most prosperous, powerful nation on Earth. Our workers are no less productive than when this crisis began. Our minds are no less inventive, our goods and services no less needed than they were last week or last month or last year.

Our capacity remains undiminished. But our time of standing pat, of protecting narrow interests and putting off unpleasant decisions—that time has surely passed. Starting today, we must pick ourselves up, dust ourselves off, and begin again the work of remaking America.

For everywhere we look, there is work to be done. The state of the economy calls for action, bold and swift, and we will act— not only to create new jobs, but to lay a new foundation for growth. We will build the roads and bridges, the electric grids and digital lines that feed our commerce and bind us together. We will restore science to its rightful place, and wield technology's wonders to raise health care's quality and lower its cost. We will harness the sun and the winds and the soil to fuel our cars and run our factories. And we will transform our schools and colleges and universities to meet the demands of a new age. All this we *can* do. And all this we *will* do.

Now, there are some who question the scale of our ambitions—who suggest that our system cannot tolerate too many big plans. Their memories are short. For they have forgotten what this country has already done, what free men and women can achieve when imagination is joined to common purpose, and necessity to courage.

What the cynics fail to understand is that the ground has shifted beneath them, that the stale political arguments that have consumed us for so long no longer apply.

The question we ask today is not whether our government is too big or too small, but whether it works—whether it helps families find jobs at a decent wage, care they can afford, a retirement that is dignified. Where the answer is yes, we intend to move forward. Where the answer is no, programs will end. And those of us who manage the public's dollars will be held to account to spend wisely, reform bad habits, and do our business in the light of day—because only then can we restore the vital trust between a people and their government.

Nor is the question before us whether the market is a force for good or ill. Its power to generate wealth and expand freedom is unmatched, but this crisis has reminded us that without a watchful eye, the market can spin out of control. The nation cannot prosper long when it favors only the prosperous. The success of our economy has always depended not just on the size of our gross domestic product, but on the reach of our prosperity—on the ability to extend opportunity to every willing heart—not out of charity, but because it is the surest route to our common good.

As for our common defense, we reject as false the choice between our safety and our ideals. Our Founding Fathers, faced with perils we can scarcely imagine, drafted a charter to assure the rule of law and the rights of man. A charter expanded by the blood of generations. Those ideals still light the world, and we will not give them up for expedience's sake.

And so to all other peoples and governments who are watching today, from the grandest capitals to the small village where my father was born: know that America is a friend of each nation and every man, woman and child who seeks a future of peace and dignity, and we are ready to lead once more.

Recall that earlier generations faced down fascism and communism not just with missiles and tanks, but with sturdy alliances and enduring convictions. They understood that our power alone cannot protect us, nor does it entitle us to do as we please. Instead, they knew that our power grows through its prudent use. Our security emanates from the justness of our cause, the force of our example, the tempering qualities of humility and restraint.

We are the keepers of this legacy. Guided by these principles once more, we can meet those new threats that demand even greater effort, even greater cooperation and understanding between nations. We will begin to responsibly leave Iraq to its people and forge a hard earned peace in Afghanistan.

With old friends and former foes, we will work tirelessly to lessen the nuclear threat and roll back the specter of a warming planet. We will not apologize for our way of life, nor will we waver in its defense.

And for those who seek to advance their aims by inducing terror and slaughtering innocents, we say to you now that our spirit is stronger and cannot be broken. You cannot outlast us, and we will defeat you.

For we know that our patchwork heritage is a strength, not a weakness. We are a nation of Christians and Muslims, Jews and Hindus, and nonbelievers. We are shaped by every language and culture, drawn from every end of this Earth. And because we have tasted the bitter swill of civil war and segregation, and emerged from that dark chapter stronger and more united, we cannot help but believe that the old hatreds shall someday pass, that the lines of tribe shall soon dissolve, that as the world grows smaller, our common humanity shall reveal itself, and that America must play its role in ushering in a new era of peace.

To the Muslim world: we seek a new way forward, based on mutual interest and mutual respect. To those leaders around the globe who seek to sow conflict, or blame their society's ills on the West: know that your people will judge you on what you can build, not what you destroy. To those who cling to power through corruption and deceit and the silencing of dissent: know that you are on the wrong side of history; but that we will extend a hand if you are willing to unclench your fist.

To the people of poor nations: we pledge to work alongside you to make your farms flourish and let clean waters flow, to nourish starved bodies and feed hungry minds. And to those nations like ours that enjoy relative plenty: we say we can no longer afford indifference to the suffering outside our borders; nor can we consume the world's resources without

THE VOICE THAT CHANGED A NATION

regard to effect. For the world has changed, and we must change with it.

As we consider the road that unfolds before us, we remember with humble gratitude those brave Americans who, at this very hour, patrol far-off deserts and distant mountains. They have something to tell us, just as the fallen heroes who lie in Arlington whisper through the ages. We honor them not only because they are guardians of our liberty, but because they embody the spirit of service, a willingness to find meaning in something greater than themselves. And yet, at this moment, a moment that will define a generation, it is precisely this spirit that must inhabit us *all*.

For as much as government can do and must do, it is ultimately the faith and determination of the American people upon which this nation relies. It is the kindness to take in a stranger when the levees break, the selflessness of workers who would rather cut their hours than see a friend lose their job which sees us through our darkest hours. It is the firefighter's courage to storm a stairway filled with smoke, but also a parent's willingness to nurture a child, that finally decides our fate.

Our challenges may be new. The instruments with which we meet them may be new. But those values upon which our success depends—honesty and hard work, courage and fair play, tolerance and curiosity, loyalty and patriotism—these things are old. These things are true. They have been the quiet force of progress throughout our history.

What is demanded then, is a return to these truths. What is required of us now, is a new era of responsibility—a recognition on the part of every American that we have duties to ourselves, our nation, and the world. Duties that we do not grudgingly accept but rather seize gladly, firm in the knowledge that there is nothing so satisfying to the spirit, so defining of our character, than giving our all to a difficult task.

This is the price and the promise of citizenship.

This is the source of our confidence—the knowledge that God calls on us to shape an uncertain destiny.

This is the meaning of our liberty and our creed—why men and women and children of every race and every faith can join in celebration across this magnificent Mall, and why a man whose father less than 60 years ago might not have been served at a local restaurant can now stand before you to take a most sacred oath.

So let us mark this day with remembrance, of who we are and how far we have traveled. In the year of America's birth, in the coldest of months, a small band of patriots huddled by dying campfires on the shores of an icy river. The capital was abandoned. The enemy was advancing. The snow was stained with blood. At a moment when the outcome of our revolution was most in doubt, the father of our nation ordered these words be read to the people:

'Let it be told to the future world, that in the depth of winter, when nothing but hope and virtue could survive... that the city and the country, alarmed at one common danger, came forth to meet [it].'

America:

In the face of our common dangers, in this winter of our hardship, let us remember these timeless words. With hope and virtue, let us brave once more the icy currents, and endure what storms may come. Let it be said by our children's children that when we were tested, we refused to let this journey end, that we did not turn back, nor did we falter; and with eyes fixed on the horizon and God's grace upon us, we carried forth that great gift of freedom and delivered it safely to future generations.

Thank you. God bless you.

And God bless the United States of America."

Economic Address

Joint Session of Congress
February 24th, 2009

I've come here tonight not only to address the distinguished men and women in this great chamber, but to speak frankly and directly to the men and women who sent us here.

I know that for many Americans watching right now, the state of our economy is a concern that rises above all others. And rightly so. If you haven't been personally affected by this recession, you probably know someone who has—a friend, a neighbor, a member of your family.

You don't need to hear another list of statistics to know that our economy is in crisis, because you live it every day. It's the worry you wake up with and the source of sleepless nights. It's the job you thought you'd retire from but now have lost; the business you built your dreams upon that's now hanging by a thread; the college acceptance letter your child had to put back in the envelope.

The impact of this recession is real, and it is everywhere.

But while our economy may be weakened and our confidence shaken, though we are living through difficult and uncertain times, tonight I want every American to know this:

We will rebuild, we will recover, and the United States of America will emerge stronger than before.

The weight of this crisis will not determine the destiny of this nation. The answers to our problems don't lie beyond our reach. They exist in our laboratories and universities, in our fields and our factories; in the imaginations of our entrepreneurs, and the pride of the hardest-working people on Earth. Those qualities that have made America the greatest force of progress and prosperity in human history, we still possess in ample measure. What is required now is for this country to pull together, confront boldly the challenges we face, and take responsibility for our future once more.

Now, if we're honest with ourselves, we'll admit that for too long, we have not always met these responsibilities—as a government or as a people. I say this not to lay blame or look backwards, but because it is only by understanding how we arrived at this moment that we'll be able to lift ourselves out of this predicament.

The fact is, our economy did not fall into decline overnight. Nor did all of our problems begin when the housing market collapsed or the stock market sank. We have known for decades that our survival depends on finding new sources of energy. Yet we import more oil today than ever before. The cost of health care eats up more and more of our savings each year, yet we keep delaying reform.

Our children will compete for jobs in a global economy that too many of our schools do not prepare them for. And though all these challenges went unsolved, we still managed to spend more money and pile up more debt, both as individuals and through our government, than ever before.

In other words, we have lived through an era where too often, short-term gains were prized over long-term prosperity; where we failed to look beyond the next payment, the next quarter,

THE VOICE THAT CHANGED A NATION

or the next election. A surplus became an excuse to transfer wealth to the wealthy instead of an opportunity to invest in our future. Regulations were gutted for the sake of a quick profit at the expense of a healthy market. People bought homes they knew they couldn't afford from banks and lenders who pushed those bad loans anyway. And all the while, critical debates and difficult decisions were put off for some other time on some other day.

Well that day of reckoning has arrived, and the time to take charge of our future is here.

Now is the time to act boldly and wisely—to not only revive this economy, but to build a new foundation for lasting prosperity. Now is the time to jumpstart job creation, re-start lending, and invest in areas like energy, health care, and education that will grow our economy, even as we make hard choices to bring our deficit down. That is what my economic agenda is designed to do, and that's what I'd like to talk to you about tonight.

It's an agenda that begins with jobs.

As soon as I took office, I asked this Congress to send me a recovery plan by President's Day that would put people back to work and put money in their pockets. Not because I believe in bigger government—I don't. Not because I'm not mindful of the massive debt we've inherited—I am.

I called for action because the failure to do so would have cost more jobs and caused more hardships. In fact, a failure to act would have worsened our long-term deficit by assuring weak economic growth for years. That's why I pushed for quick action. And tonight, I am grateful that this Congress delivered, and pleased to say that the American Recovery and Reinvestment Act is now law.

Over the next two years, this plan will save or create 3.5 million jobs. More than 90% of these jobs will be in the private sector—jobs rebuilding our roads and bridges; constructing wind turbines and solar panels; laying broadband and expanding mass transit.

Because of this plan, there are teachers who can now keep their jobs and educate our kids. Health care professionals can continue caring for our sick. There are fifty-seven police officers who are still on the streets of Minneapolis tonight because this plan prevented the layoffs their department was about to make.

Because of this plan, 95% of the working households in America will receive a tax cut—a tax cut that you will see in your paychecks beginning on April 1st.

Because of this plan, families who are struggling to pay tuition costs will receive a $2,500 tax credit for all four years of college. And Americans who have lost their jobs in this recession will be able to receive extended unemployment benefits and continued health care coverage to help them weather this storm.

I know there are some in this chamber and watching at home who are skeptical of whether this plan will work. I understand that skepticism. Here in Washington, we've all seen how quickly good intentions can turn into broken promises and wasteful spending. And with a plan of this scale comes enormous responsibility to get it right.

That is why I have asked Vice President Biden to lead a tough, unprecedented oversight effort—because nobody messes with Joe. I have told each member of my Cabinet as well as mayors and governors across the country that they will be held accountable by me and the American people for every dollar they spend. I have appointed a proven and aggressive Inspector General to ferret out any and all cases of waste and fraud. And we have created a new website called recovery.gov so that every American can find out how and where their money is being spent.

So the recovery plan we passed is the first step in getting our economy back on track. But it is just the first step. Because even if we manage this plan flawlessly, there will be no real recovery unless we clean up the credit crisis that has severely weakened our financial system.

I want to speak plainly and candidly about this issue tonight, because every American should know that it directly affects you and your family's well-being. You should also know that the money you've deposited in banks across the country is safe; your insurance is secure; and you can rely on the continued operation of our financial system. That is not the source of concern.

The concern is that if we do not re-start lending in this country, our recovery will be choked off before it even begins.

You see, the flow of credit is the lifeblood of our economy. The ability to get a loan is how you finance the purchase of everything from a home to a car to a college education—how stores stock their shelves, farms buy equipment, and businesses make payroll.

But credit has stopped flowing the way it should. Too many bad loans from the housing crisis have made their way onto the books of too many banks. With so much debt and so little confidence, these banks are now fearful of lending out any more money to households, to businesses, or to each other. When there is no lending, families can't afford to buy homes or cars.

So businesses are forced to make layoffs. Our economy suffers even more, and credit dries up even further.

That is why this administration is moving swiftly and aggressively to break this destructive cycle, restore confidence, and re-start lending.

We will do so in several ways. First, we are creating a new lending fund that represents the largest effort ever to help provide auto loans, college loans, and small business loans to the consumers and entrepreneurs who keep this economy running.

Second, we have launched a housing plan that will help responsible families facing the threat of foreclosure lower their monthly payments and re-finance their mortgages. It's a plan that won't help speculators or that neighbor down the street who bought a house he could never hope to afford, but it will help millions of Americans who are struggling with declining home values—Americans who will now be able to take advantage of the lower interest rates that this plan has already helped bring about. In fact, the average family who re-finances today can save nearly $2000 per year on their mortgage.

Third, we will act with the full force of the federal government to ensure that the major banks that Americans depend on

116   *THE VOICE THAT CHANGED A NATION*

have enough confidence and enough money to lend even in more difficult times. And when we learn that a major bank has serious problems, we will hold accountable those responsible, force the necessary adjustments, provide the support to clean up their balance sheets, and assure the continuity of a strong, viable institution that can serve our people and our economy.

I understand that on any given day, Wall Street may be more comforted by an approach that gives banks bailouts with no strings attached, and that holds nobody accountable for their reckless decisions. But such an approach won't solve the problem. And our goal is to quicken the day when we re-start lending to the American people and American business and end this crisis once and for all.

I intend to hold these banks fully accountable for the assistance they receive, and this time, they will have to clearly demonstrate how taxpayer dollars result in more lending for the American taxpayer. This time, CEOs won't be able to use taxpayer money to pad their paychecks or buy fancy drapes or disappear on a private jet. Those days are over.

Still, this plan will require significant resources from the federal government—and yes, probably more than we've already set aside. But while the cost of action will be great, I can assure you that the cost of inaction will be far greater, for it could result in an economy that sputters along for not months or years, but perhaps a decade. That would be worse for our deficit, worse for business, worse for you and worse for the next generation. And I refuse to let that happen.

I understand that when the last administration asked this Congress to provide assistance for struggling banks, Democrats and Republicans alike were infuriated by the mismanagement and results that followed. So were the American taxpayers. So was I.

So I know how unpopular it is to be seen as helping banks right now, especially when everyone is suffering in part from their bad decisions. I promise you—I get it.

But I also know that in a time of crisis, we cannot afford to govern out of anger, or yield to the politics of the moment. My job—our job—is to solve the problem. Our job is to govern with a sense of responsibility. I will not spend a single penny for the purpose of rewarding a single Wall Street executive, but I will do whatever it takes to help the small business that can't pay its workers or the family that has saved and still can't get a mortgage.

That's what this is about. It's not about helping banks—it's about helping people. Because when credit is available again, that young family can finally buy a new home. And then some company will hire workers to build it. And then those workers will have money to spend, and if they can get a loan too, maybe they'll finally buy that car, or open their own business. Investors will return to the market, and American families will see their retirement secured once more. Slowly, but surely, confidence will return and our economy will recover.

So I ask this Congress to join me in doing whatever proves necessary. Because we cannot consign our nation to an open-ended recession. And to ensure that a crisis of this magnitude never happens again, I ask Congress to move quickly on legislation that will finally reform our outdated regulatory system. It is time to put in place tough, new common-sense rules of the road so that our financial market rewards drive and innovation, and punishes short-cuts and abuse.

THE VOICE THAT CHANGED A NATION

The recovery plan and the financial stability plan are the immediate steps we're taking to revive our economy in the short-term. But the only way to fully restore America's economic strength is to make the long-term investments that will lead to new jobs, new industries, and a renewed ability to compete with the rest of the world.

The only way this century will be another American century is if we confront at last the price of our dependence on oil and the high cost of health care; the schools that aren't preparing our children and the mountain of debt they stand to inherit. That is our responsibility.

In the next few days, I will submit a budget to Congress. So often, we have come to view these documents as simply numbers on a page or laundry lists of programs. I see this document differently. I see it as a vision for America—as a blueprint for our future.

My budget does not attempt to solve every problem or address every issue. It reflects the stark reality of what we've inherited—a trillion dollar deficit, a financial crisis, and a costly recession.

Given these realities, everyone in this chamber—Democrats and Republicans—will have to sacrifice some worthy priorities for which there are no dollars. And that includes me.

But that does not mean we can afford to ignore our long-term challenges. I reject the view that says our problems will simply take care of themselves, that says government has no role in laying the foundation for our common prosperity.

For history tells a different story. History reminds us that at every moment of economic upheaval and transformation, this nation has responded with bold action and big ideas. In the midst of civil war, we laid railroad tracks from one coast to another that spurred commerce and industry. From the turmoil of the Industrial Revolution came a system of public high schools that prepared our citizens for a new age. In the wake of war and depression, the GI Bill sent a generation to college and created the largest middle class in history. And a twilight struggle for freedom led to a nation of highways, an American on the moon, and an explosion of technology that still shapes our world.

In each case, government didn't supplant private enterprise; it catalyzed private enterprise. It created the conditions for thousands of entrepreneurs and new businesses to adapt and to thrive.

We are a nation that has seen promise amid peril, and claimed opportunity from ordeal. Now we must be that nation again. That is why, even as it cuts back on the programs we don't need, the budget I submit will invest in the three areas that are absolutely critical to our economic future: energy, health care, and education.

It begins with energy.

We know the country that harnesses the power of clean, renewable energy will lead the 21st century. And yet, it is China that has launched the largest effort in history to make their economy energy efficient. We invented solar technology, but we've fallen behind countries like Germany and Japan in producing it. New plug-in hybrids roll off our assembly lines, but they will run on batteries made in Korea.

THE VOICE THAT CHANGED A NATION

Well I do not accept a future where the jobs and industries of tomorrow take root beyond our borders—and I know you don't either. It is time for America to lead again.

Thanks to our recovery plan, we will double this nation's supply of renewable energy in the next three years. We have also made the largest investment in basic research funding in American history—an investment that will spur not only new discoveries in energy, but breakthroughs in medicine, science, and technology.

We will soon lay down thousands of miles of power lines that can carry new energy to cities and towns across this country. And we will put Americans to work making our homes and buildings more efficient so that we can save billions of dollars on our energy bills.

But to truly transform our economy, protect our security, and save our planet from the ravages of climate change, we need to ultimately make clean, renewable energy the profitable kind of energy. So I ask this Congress to send me legislation that places a market-based cap on carbon pollution and drives the production of more renewable energy in America. And to support that innovation, we will invest fifteen billion dollars a year to develop technologies like wind power and solar power; advanced bio-fuels, clean coal, and more fuel efficient cars and trucks built right here in America.

As for our auto industry, everyone recognizes that years of bad decision making and a global recession have pushed our automakers to the brink. We should not, and will not, protect them from their own bad practices. But we are committed to the goal of a re-tooled, re-imagined auto industry that can compete and win. Millions of jobs depend on it. Scores of communities depend on it. And I believe the nation that invented the automobile cannot walk away from it.

None of this will come without cost, nor will it be easy. But this is America. We don't do what's easy. We do what is necessary to move this country forward.

For that same reason, we must also address the crushing cost of health care.

This is a cost that now causes a bankruptcy in America every thirty seconds. By the end of the year, it could cause 1.5 million Americans to lose their homes. In the last eight years, premiums have grown four times faster than wages. And in each of these years, one million more Americans have lost their health insurance. It is one of the major reasons why small businesses close their doors and corporations ship jobs overseas. And it's one of the largest and fastest growing parts of our budget.

Given these facts, we can no longer afford to put health care reform on hold.

Already, we have done more to advance the cause of health care reform in the last thirty days than we have in the last decade. When it was days old, this Congress passed a law to provide and protect health insurance for eleven million American children whose parents work full-time.

Our recovery plan will invest in electronic health records and new technology that will reduce errors, bring down costs, ensure privacy, and save lives. It will launch a new effort to conquer a disease that has touched the life of nearly every American by seeking a cure for cancer in our time. And it makes the largest investment ever in preventive care, because that is one of the best ways to keep our people healthy and our costs under control.

This budget builds on these reforms. It includes an historic commitment to comprehensive health care reform—a down payment on the principle that we must have quality, affordable health care for every American. It's a commitment that's paid for in part by efficiencies in our system that are long overdue. And it's a step we must take if we hope to bring down our deficit in the years to come.

Now, there will be many different opinions and ideas about how to achieve reform, and that is why I'm bringing together businesses and workers, doctors and health care providers, Democrats and Republicans to begin work on this issue next week.

I suffer no illusions that this will be an easy process. It will be hard. But I also know that nearly a century after Teddy Roosevelt first called for reform, the cost of our health care has weighed down our economy and the conscience of our nation long enough. So let there be no doubt: health care reform cannot wait. It must not wait and it will not wait another year.

The third challenge we must address is the urgent need to expand the promise of education in America.

In a global economy where the most valuable skill you can sell is your knowledge, a good education is no longer just a pathway to opportunity—it is a pre-requisite.

Right now, three-quarters of the fastest growing occupations require more than a high school diploma. And yet, just over half of our citizens have that level of education. We have one of the highest high school dropout rates of any industrialized nation. And half of the students who begin college never finish.

This is a prescription for economic decline, because we know the countries that out-teach us today will out-compete us tomorrow. That is why it will be the goal of this administration to ensure that every child has access to a complete and competitive education—from the day they are born to the day they begin a career.

Already, we have made an historic investment in education through the economic recovery plan. We have dramatically expanded early childhood education and will continue to improve its quality, because we know that the most formative learning comes in those first years of life.

We have made college affordable for nearly seven million more students. And we have provided the resources necessary to prevent painful cuts and teacher layoffs that would set back our children's progress.

But we know that our schools don't just need more resources. They need more reform. That is why this budget creates new incentives for teacher performance, pathways for advancement, and rewards for success. We'll invest in innovative programs that are already helping schools meet high standards and close achievement gaps. And we will expand our commitment to charter schools.

It is our responsibility as lawmakers and educators to make this system work. But it is the responsibility of every citizen to participate in it. And so tonight, I ask every American to commit to at least one year or more of higher education or career training. This can be community college or a four year school, vocational training or an apprenticeship.

But whatever the training may be, every American will need to get more than a high school diploma. And dropping out of high school is no longer an option. It's not just quitting on yourself, it's quitting on your country—and this country needs and values the talents of every American.

That is why we will provide the support necessary for you to complete college and meet a new goal: by 2020, America will once again have the highest proportion of college graduates in the world.

I know that the price of tuition is higher than ever, which is why if you are willing to volunteer in your neighborhood or give back to your community or serve your country, we will make sure that you can afford a higher education. And to encourage a renewed spirit of national service for this and future generations, I ask this Congress to send me the bipartisan legislation that bears the name of Senator Orrin Hatch as well as an American who has never stopped asking what he can do for his country—Senator Edward Kennedy.

These education policies will open the doors of opportunity for our children. But it is up to us to ensure they walk through them. In the end, there is no program or policy that can substitute for a mother or father who will attend those parent/teacher conferences, or help with homework after dinner, or turn off the TV, put away the video games, and read to their child. I speak to you not just as a President, but as a father when I say that responsibility for our children's education must begin at home.

There is, of course, another responsibility we have to our children. And that is the responsibility to ensure that we do not pass on to them a debt they cannot pay. With the deficit we inherited, the cost of the crisis we face, and the long-term challenges we must meet, it has never been more important to ensure that as our economy recovers, we do what it takes to bring this deficit down.

I'm proud that we passed the recovery plan free of earmarks, and I want to pass a budget next year that ensures that each dollar we spend reflects only our most important national priorities.

Yesterday, I held a fiscal summit where I pledged to cut the deficit in half by the end of my first term in office. My administration has also begun to go line by line through the federal budget in order to eliminate wasteful and ineffective programs. As you can imagine, this is a process that will take some time. But we're starting with the biggest lines. We have already identified two trillion dollars in savings over the next decade.

In this budget, we will end education programs that don't work and end direct payments to large agri-businesses that don't need them. We'll eliminate the no-bid contracts that have wasted billions in Iraq, and reform our defense budget so that we're not paying for Cold War era weapons systems we don't use. We will root out the waste, fraud, and abuse in our Medicare program that doesn't make our seniors any healthier, and we will restore a sense of fairness and balance to our tax code by finally ending the tax breaks for corporations that ship our jobs overseas.

In order to save our children from a future of debt, we will also end the tax breaks for the wealthiest 2% of Americans.

But let me perfectly clear, because I know you'll hear the same old claims that rolling back these tax breaks means a massive tax increase on the American people: if your family earns less than $250,000 a year, you will not see your taxes increased a single dime. I repeat: not one single dime. In fact, the recovery plan provides a tax cut—that's right, a tax cut—for 95% of working families. And these checks are on the way.

To preserve our long-term fiscal health, we must also address the growing costs in Medicare and Social Security.

Comprehensive health care reform is the best way to strengthen Medicare for years to come. And we must also begin a conversation on how to do the same for Social Security, while creating tax free universal savings accounts for all Americans.

Finally, because we're also suffering from a deficit of trust, I am committed to restoring a sense of honesty and accountability to our budget. That is why this budget looks ahead ten years and accounts for spending that was left out under the old rules—and for the first time, that includes the full cost of fighting in Iraq and Afghanistan. For seven years, we have been a nation at war. No longer will we hide its price.

We are now carefully reviewing our policies in both wars, and I will soon announce a way forward in Iraq that leaves Iraq to its people and responsibly ends this war.

And with our friends and allies, we will forge a new and comprehensive strategy for Afghanistan and Pakistan to defeat al Qaeda and combat extremism. Because I will not allow terrorists to plot against the American people from safe havens half a world away.

As we meet here tonight, our men and women in uniform stand watch abroad and more are readying to deploy. To each and every one of them, and to the families who bear the quiet burden of their absence, Americans are united in sending one message: we honor your service, we are inspired by your sacrifice, and you have our unyielding support.

To relieve the strain on our forces, my budget increases the number of our soldiers and Marines. And to keep our sacred trust with those who serve, we will raise their pay, and give our veterans the expanded health care and benefits that they have earned.

To overcome extremism, we must also be vigilant in upholding the values our troops defend—because there is no force in the world more powerful than the example of America. That is why I have ordered the closing of the detention center at Guantanamo Bay, and will seek swift and certain justice for captured terrorists—because living our values doesn't make us weaker, it makes us safer and it makes us stronger.

And that is why I can stand here tonight and say without exception or equivocation that the United States of America does not torture.

In words and deeds, we are showing the world that a new era of engagement has begun. For we know that America cannot meet the threats of this century alone, but the world cannot meet them without America. We cannot shun the negotiating table, nor ignore the foes or forces that could do us harm.

We are instead called to move forward with the sense of confidence and candor that serious times demand.

To seek progress toward a secure and lasting peace between Israel and her neighbors, we have appointed an envoy to sustain our effort. To meet the challenges of the 21st century—from terrorism to nuclear proliferation, from pandemic disease to cyber threats to crushing poverty—we will strengthen old alliances, forge new ones, and use all elements of our national power.

And to respond to an economic crisis that is global in scope, we are working with the nations of the G-20 to restore confidence in our financial system, avoid the possibility of escalating protectionism, and spur demand for American goods in markets across the globe. For the world depends on us to have a strong economy, just as our economy depends on the strength of the world's.

As we stand at this crossroads of history, the eyes of all people in all nations are once again upon us—watching to see what we do with this moment, waiting for us to lead.

Those of us gathered here tonight have been called to govern in extraordinary times. It is a tremendous burden, but also a great privilege—one that has been entrusted to few generations of Americans. For in our hands lies the ability to shape our world for good or for ill.

I know that it is easy to lose sight of this truth—to become cynical and doubtful, consumed with the petty and the trivial.

But in my life, I have also learned that hope is found in unlikely places; that inspiration often comes not from those with the most power or celebrity, but from the dreams and aspirations of Americans who are anything but ordinary.

I think about Leonard Abess, the bank president from Miami who reportedly cashed out of his company, took a $60 million bonus, and gave it out to all 399 people who worked for him, plus another seventy-two who used to work for him. He didn't tell anyone, but when the local newspaper found out, he simply said, "I knew some of these people since I was 7 years old. I didn't feel right getting the money myself."

I think about Greensburg, Kansas, a town that was completely destroyed by a tornado, but is being rebuilt by its residents as a global example of how clean energy can power an entire community—how it can bring jobs and businesses to a place where piles of bricks and rubble once lay.

"The tragedy was terrible," said one of the men who helped them rebuild. "But the folks here know that it also provided an incredible opportunity."

And I think about Ty'Sheoma Bethea, the young girl from that school I visited in Dillon, South Carolina—a place where the ceilings leak, the paint peels off the walls, and they have to stop teaching six times a day because the train barrels by their classroom. She has been told that her school is hopeless, but the other day after class, she went to the public library and typed up a letter to the people sitting in this room. She even asked her principal for the money to buy a stamp.

The letter asks us for help, and says, "We are just students trying to become lawyers, doctors, congressmen like yourself and one day president, so we can make a change to not just the state of South Carolina but also the world. We are not quitters."

We are not quitters.

These words and these stories tell us something about the spirit of the people who sent us here. They tell us that even in the most trying times, amid the most difficult circumstances, there is a generosity, a resilience, a decency, and a determination that perseveres—a willingness to take responsibility for our future and for posterity.

Their resolve must be our inspiration. Their concerns must be our cause. And we must show them and all our people that we are equal to the task before us.

I know that we haven't agreed on every issue thus far, and there are surely times in the future when we will part ways. But I also know that every American who is sitting here tonight loves this country and wants it to succeed.

That must be the starting point for every debate we have in the coming months, and where we return after those debates are done. That is the foundation on which the American people expect us to build common ground.

And if we do—if we come together and lift this nation from the depths of this crisis, if we put our people back to work and restart the engine of our prosperity, if we confront without fear the challenges of our time and summon that enduring spirit of an America that does not quit—then someday years from now our children can tell their children that this was the time when we performed, in the words that are carved into this very chamber, "something worthy to be remembered."

Thank you. God Bless you, and may God Bless the United States of America.

Against the Iraq War

The Federal Plaza in Chicago, Illinois
October 2002

I stand before you as someone who is not opposed to war in all circumstances. The Civil War was one of the bloodiest in history, and yet it was only through the crucible of the sword, the sacrifice of multitudes, that we could begin to perfect this union and drive the scourge of slavery from our soil.

I don't oppose all wars. My grandfather signed up for a war the day after Pearl Harbor was bombed, fought in Patton's army. He fought in the name of a larger freedom, part of that arsenal of democracy that triumphed over evil.

I don't oppose all wars.

After September 11, after witnessing the carnage and destruction, the dust and the tears, I supported this administration's pledge to hunt down and root out those who would slaughter innocents in the name of intolerance, and I would willingly take up arms myself to prevent such tragedy from happening again.

I don't oppose all wars. What I am opposed to is a dumb war. What I am opposed to is a rash war. What I am opposed to is the cynical attempt by Richard Perle and Paul Wolfowitz and other armchair, weekend warriors in this administration to shove their own ideological agendas down our throats, irrespective of the costs in lives lost and in hardships borne.

What I am opposed to is the attempt by political hacks like Karl Rove to distract us from a rise in the uninsured, a rise in the poverty rate, a drop in the median income, to distract us from corporate scandals and a stock market that has just gone through the worst month since the Great Depression.

That's what I'm opposed to. A dumb war. A rash war. A war based not on reason but on passion, not on principle but on politics.

Now let me be clear: I suffer no illusions about Saddam Hussein. He is a brutal man. A ruthless man. A man who butchers his own people to secure his own power. The world, and the Iraqi people, would be better off without him.

But I also know that Saddam poses no imminent and direct threat to the United States, or to his neighbor, and that in concert with the international community he can be contained until, in the way of all petty dictators, he falls away into the dustbin of history.

I know that even a successful war against Iraq will require a U.S. occupation of undetermined length, at undetermined cost, with undetermined consequences.

I know that an invasion of Iraq without a clear rationale and without strong international support will only fan the flames of the Middle East, and encourage the worst, rather than best, impulses of the Arab world, and strengthen the recruitment arm of al-Qaeda.

I am not opposed to all wars. I'm opposed to dumb wars. So for those of us who seek a more just and secure world for our children, let us send a clear message to the president.

You want a fight, President Bush? Let's finish the fight with Bin Laden and al-Qaeda, through effective, coordinated intelligence, and a shutting down of the financial networks that support terrorism, and a homeland security program that involves more than color-coded warnings.

You want a fight, President Bush? Let's fight to make sure that we vigorously enforce a nonproliferation treaty, and that former enemies and current allies like Russia safeguard and ultimately eliminate their stores of nuclear material, and that nations like Pakistan and India never use the terrible weapons already in their possession, and that the arms merchants in our own country stop feeding the countless wars that rage across the globe.

You want a fight, President Bush? Let's fight to make sure our so-called allies in the Middle East, the Saudis and the Egyptians, stop oppressing their own people, and suppressing dissent, and tolerating corruption and inequality, and mismanaging their economies so that their youth grow up without education, without prospects, without hope, the ready recruits of terrorist cells.

You want a fight, President Bush? Let's fight to wean ourselves off Middle East oil through an energy policy that doesn't simply serve the interests of Exxon and Mobil.

Those are the battles that we need to fight. Those are the battles that we willingly join. The battles against ignorance and intolerance, corruption and greed, poverty and despair.

The consequences of war are dire, the sacrifices immeasurable. We may have occasion in our lifetime to once again rise up in defense of our freedom, and pay the wages of war. But we ought not—we will not—travel down that hellish path blindly. Nor should we allow those who would march off and pay the ultimate sacrifice, who would prove the full measure of devotion with their blood, to make such an awful sacrifice in vain.

Father's Day Speech

Apostolic Church of God
Chicago, Illinois
June 15th, 2008

Good morning. It's good to be home on this Father's Day with my girls, and it's an honor to spend some time with all of you today in the house of our Lord.

At the end of the Sermon on the Mount, Jesus closes by saying, "Whoever hears these words of mine, and does them, shall be likened to a wise man who built his house upon a rock: the rain descended, and the floods came, and the winds blew, and beat upon that house, and it fell not, for it was founded upon a rock." (Matthew 7: 24-25)

...Of all the rocks upon which we build our lives, we are reminded today that family is the most important. And we are called to recognize and honor how critical every father is to that foundation. They are teachers and coaches. They are mentors and role models. They are examples of success and the men who constantly push us toward it.

But if we are honest with ourselves, we'll admit that what too many fathers also are missing—missing from too many lives and too many homes. They have abandoned their responsibilities, acting like boys instead of men. And the foundations of our families are weaker because of it.

You and I know how true this is in the African-American community. We know that more than half of all black children live in single parent households, a number that has doubled—doubled—since we were children.

We know the statistics—that children who grow up without a father are five times more likely to live in poverty and commit crime, nine times more likely to drop out of schools, and twenty times more likely to end up in prison. They are more likely to have behavioral problems, or run away from home, or become teenage parents themselves. And the foundations of our community are weaker because of it.

How many times in the last year has this city lost a child at the hands of another child? How many times have our hearts stopped in the middle of the night with the sound of a gunshot or a siren? How many teenagers have we seen hanging around on street corners when they should be sitting in a classroom? How many are sitting in prison when they should b working, or at least looking for a job? How many in this generation are we willing to lose to poverty or violence or addiction? How many?

Yes, we need more cops on the street. Yes, we need fewer guns in the hands of people who shouldn't have them. Yes, we need more money for our schools, and more outstanding teachers in the classroom, and more afterschool programs for our children. Yes, we need more jobs and more job training and more opportunity in our communities.

But we also need families to raise our children. We need fathers to realize that responsibility does not end at conception. We need them to realize that what makes you a man is not the ability to have a child—it's the courage to raise one.

We need to help all the mothers out there who are raising these kids by themselves—the mothers who drop them off at school, go to work, pick up them up in the afternoon, work another shift, get dinner, make lunches, pay the bills, fix the house, and all the other things it takes both parents to do. So many of these women are doing a heroic job, but they need support. They need another parent. Their children need another parent. That's what keeps their foundation strong. It's what keeps the foundation of our country strong.

I know what it means to have an absent father, although my circumstances weren't as tough as they are for many young people today. Even though my father left us when I was two years old, and I only knew him from the letters he wrote and the stories that my family told, I was luckier than most.

I grew up in Hawaii and had two wonderful grandparents from Kansas who poured everything they had into helping my mother raise my sister and me—who worked with her to teach us about love and respect and the obligations we have to one another.

I screwed up more often than I should've, but I got plenty of second chances. And even though we didn't have a lot of money, scholarships gave me the opportunity to go to some of the best schools in the country. A lot of kids don't get these chances today. There is no margin for error in their lives. So my own story is different in that way.

Still, I know the toll that being a single parent took on my mother—how she struggled at times to the pay bills, to give us the things that other kids had, to play all the roles that both parents are supposed to play. And I know the toll it took on me.

So I resolved many years ago that it was my obligation to break the cycle—that if I could be anything in life, I would be a good father to my girls; that if I could give them anything, I would give them that rock—that foundation—on which to build their lives. And that would be the greatest gift I could offer.

I say this knowing that I have been an imperfect father— knowing that I have made mistakes and will continue to make more; wishing that I could be home for my girls and my wife more than I am right now. I say this knowing all of these things because even as we are imperfect, even as we face difficult circumstances, there are still certain lessons we must strive to live and learn as fathers—whether we are black or white, rich or poor, from the South Side or the wealthiest suburb.

The first is setting an example of excellence for our children— because if we want to set high expectations for them, we've got to set high expectations for ourselves.

It's great if you have a job; it's even better if you have a college degree. It's a wonderful thing if you are married and living in a home with your children, but don't just sit in the house and watch Sports Center all weekend long. That's why so many children are growing up in front of the television. As fathers and parents, we've got to spend more time with them, and help them with their homework, and replace the video game or the remote control with a book once in awhile. That's how we build that foundation.

We know that education is everything to our children's future. We know that they will no longer just compete for good jobs with children from Indiana, but children from India and China and all over the world. We know the work and the studying and the level of education that requires.

You know, sometimes I'll go to an eighth-grade graduation and there's all that pomp and circumstance and gowns and flowers. And I think to myself, it's just eighth grade. To really compete, they need to graduate high school, and then they need to graduate college, and they probably need a graduate degree too. An eighth-grade education doesn't cut it today. Let's give them a handshake and tell them to get their butts back in the library!

It's up to us—as fathers and parents—to instill this ethic of excellence in our children. It's up to us to say to our daughters, don't ever let images on TV tell you what you are worth, because I expect you to dream without limit and reach for those goals.

It's up to us to tell our sons, those songs on the radio may glorify violence, but in my house we give glory to achievement, self respect, and hard work. It's up to us to set these high expectations. And that means meeting those expectations ourselves. That means setting examples of excellence in our own lives.

The second thing we need to do as fathers is pass along the value of empathy to our children. Not sympathy, but empathy—the ability to stand in somebody else's shoes, to look at the world through their eyes. Sometimes it's so easy to get caught up in "us," that we forget about our obligations to one another. There's a culture in our society that says remembering these obligations is somehow soft—that we can't show weakness, and so therefore we can't show kindness.

But our young boys and girls see that. They see when you are ignoring or mistreating your wife. They see when you are inconsiderate at home, or when you are distant, or when you are thinking only of yourself. And so it's no surprise when we see that behavior in our schools or on our streets.

That's why we pass on the values of empathy and kindness to our children by living them. We need to show our kids that you're not strong by putting other people down—you're strong by lifting them up. That's our responsibility as fathers.

And by the way—it's a responsibility that also extends to Washington. Because if fathers are doing their part—if they're taking our responsibilities seriously to be there for their children, and set high expectations for them, and instill in them a sense of excellence and empathy, then our government should meet them halfway.

We should be making it easier for fathers who make responsible choices and harder for those who avoid them. We should get rid of the financial penalties we impose on married couples right now, and start making sure that every dime of child support goes directly to helping children instead of some bureaucrat. We should reward fathers who pay that child support with job training and job opportunities and a larger Earned Income Tax Credit that can help them pay the bills.

We should expand programs where registered nurses visit expectant and new mothers and help them learn how to care for themselves before the baby is born and what to do after—programs that have helped increase father involvement, women's employment, and children's readiness for school. We should help these new families care for their children by

THE VOICE THAT CHANGED A NATION

expanding maternity and paternity leave. And we should guarantee every worker more paid sick leave so they can stay home to take care of their child without losing their income.

We should take all of these steps to build a strong foundation for our children. But we should also know that even if we do— even if we meet our obligations as fathers and parents—even if Washington does its part too, we will still face difficult challenges in our lives. There will still be days of struggle and heartache. The rains will still come and the winds will still blow.

And that is why the final lesson we must learn as fathers is also the greatest gift we can pass on to our children—and that is the gift of hope.

I'm not talking about an idle hope that's little more than blind optimism or willful ignorance of the problems we face. I'm talking about hope as that spirit inside us that insists, despite all evidence to the contrary, that something better is waiting for us if we're willing to work for it and fight for it, if we are willing to believe.

I was answering questions at a town hall meeting in Wisconsin the other day and a young man raised his hand, and I figured he'd ask about college tuition or energy or maybe the war in Iraq. But instead, he looked at me very seriously and he asked, "What does life mean to you?"

Now, I have to admit that I wasn't quite prepared for that one. I think I stammered for a little bit, but then I stopped and gave it some thought, and I said this:

When I was a young man, I thought life was all about me—how do I make my way in the world, and how do I become successful, and how do I get the things that I want.

But now, my life revolves around my two little girls. And what I think about is what kind of world I'm leaving them.

Are they living in a county where there's a huge gap between a few who are wealthy and a whole bunch of people who are struggling every day? Are they living in a county that is still divided by race? A country where, because they're girls, they don't have as much opportunity as boys do? Are they living in a country where we are hated around the world because we don't cooperate effectively with other nations? Are they living a world that is in grave danger because of what we've done to its climate?

And what I've realized is that life doesn't count for much unless you're willing to do your small part to leave our children—all of our children—a better world. Even if it's difficult. Even if the work seems great. Even if we don't get very far in our lifetime.

That is our ultimate responsibility as fathers and parents. We try. We hope.

We do what we can to build our house upon the sturdiest rock. And when the winds come, and the rains fall, and they beat upon that house—we keep faith that our Father will be there to guide us, and watch over us, and protect us, and lead His children through the darkest of storms into light of a better day. That is my prayer for all of us on this Father's Day, and that is my hope for this country in the years ahead.

May God Bless you and your children. Thank you.

Habeas Corpus Amendment

Senate Floor Statement
September 27, 2006

Mr. President, I would like to address the habeas corpus amendment that is on the floor and that we just heard a lengthy debate about between Senator Specter and Senator Warner.

A few years ago, I gave a speech in Boston that people talk about from time to time. In that speech, I spoke about why I love this country, why I love America, and what I believe sets this country apart from so many other nations in so many areas. I said:

"That is the true genius of America—a faith in simple dreams, an insistence on small miracles; that we can tuck in our children at night and know that they are fed and clothed and safe from harm; that we can say what we think, write what we think, without hearing a sudden knock on the door."

Without hearing a sudden knock on the door. I bring this up because what is at stake in this bill and in the amendment that is currently being debated, is the right—in some sense, for people who hear that knock on the door and are placed in detention because the Government suspects them of terrorist activity—to effectively challenge their detention by our Government.

Now, under the existing rules of the Detainee Treatment Act, court review of anyone's detention is severely restricted. Fortunately, the Supreme Court in Hamdan ensured that some

145

meaningful review would take place. But in the absence of Senator Specter's amendment that is currently pending, we will essentially be going back to the same situation as if the Supreme Court had never ruled in Hamdan; a situation in which detainees effectively have no access to anything other than the Combatant Status Review Tribunal, or the CSRT.

Now, I think it is important for all of us to understand exactly the procedures that are currently provided for under the CSRT. I have actually read a few of the transcripts of proceedings under the CSRT. And I can tell you that often-times they provide detainees no meaningful recourse if the Government has the wrong guy.

Essentially, reading these transcripts, they proceed as follows. The Government says: You are a member of the Taliban. And the detainee will say: No, I'm not. And then the Government will not ask for proof from the detainee that he is not. There is no evidence that the detainee can offer to rebut the Government's charge.

The Government then moves on and says: And on such and such a date, you perpetrated such and such terrorist crime. And the detainee says: No, I didn't. You have the wrong guy. But again, he has no capacity to place into evidence anything that would rebut the Government's charge. And there is no effort to find out whether or not what he is saying is true.

And it proceeds like that until effectively the Government says, OK, that is the end of the tribunal, and he goes back to detention. Even if there is evidence that he was not involved in any terrorist activity, he may not have any mechanism to introduce that evidence into the hearing.

Now, the vast majority of the folks in Guantanamo, I suspect, are there for a reason. There are a lot of dangerous people. Particularly dangerous are people like Khalid Shaikh Mohammed. Ironically, those are the guys who are going to get real military procedures because they are going to be charged by the Government. But detainees who have not committed war crimes—or where the Government's case is not strong—may not have any recourse whatsoever.

The bottom line is this: Current procedures under the CSRT are such that a perfectly innocent individual could be held and could not rebut the Government's case and has no way of proving his innocence.

I would like somebody in this Chamber, somebody in this Government, to tell me why this is necessary. I do not want to hear that this is a new world and we face a new kind of enemy. I know that. I know that every time I think about my two little girls and worry for their safety—when I wonder if I really can tuck them in at night and know that they are safe from harm. I have as big of a stake as anybody on the other side of the aisle and anybody in this administration in capturing terrorists and incapacitating them. I would gladly take up arms myself against any terrorist threat to make sure my family is protected.

But as a parent, I can also imagine the terror I would feel if one of my family members were rounded up in the middle of the night and sent to Guantanamo without even getting one chance to ask why they were being held and being able to prove their innocence.

This is not just an entirely fictional scenario, by the way. We have already had reports by the CIA and various generals over the last few years saying that many of the detainees at Guantanamo should not have been there.

As one U.S. commander of Guantanamo told the Wall Street Journal, "Sometimes, we just didn't get the right folks."

We all know about the recent case of the Canadian man who was suspected of terrorist connections, detained in New York, sent to Syria—through a rendition agreement—tortured, only to find out later it was all a case of mistaken identity and poor information.

In this war, where terrorists can plot undetected from within our borders, it is absolutely vital that our law enforcement agencies are able to detain and interrogate whoever they believe to be a suspect, and so it is understandable that mistakes will be made and identities will be confused. I don't blame the Government for that. This is an extraordinarily difficult war we are prosecuting against terrorists. There are going to be situations in which we cast too wide a net and capture the wrong person.

But what is avoidable is refusing to ever allow our legal system to correct these mistakes. By giving suspects a chance—even one chance—to challenge the terms of their detention in court, to have a judge confirm that the Government has detained the right person for the right suspicions, we could solve this problem without harming our efforts in the war on terror one bit.

Let me respond to a couple of points that have been made on the other side. You will hear opponents of this amendment say it will give all kinds of rights to terrorist masterminds, such as Khalid Shaikh Mohammed. But that is not true. The irony of the underlying bill as it is written is that someone like

Khalid Shaikh Mohammed is going to get basically a full military trial, with all of the bells and whistles. He will have counsel, he will be able to present evidence, and he will be able to rebut the Government's case.

The feeling is that he is guilty of a war crime and to do otherwise might violate some of our agreements under the Geneva Conventions. I think that is good, that we are going to provide him with some procedure and process. I think we will convict him, and I think he will be brought to justice. I think justice will be carried out in his case.

But that won't be true for the detainees who are never charged with a terrorist crime, who have not committed a war crime. Under this bill, people who may have been simply at the wrong place at the wrong time—and there may be just a few— will never get a chance to appeal their detention. So, essentially, the weaker the Government's case is against you, the fewer rights you have. Senator Specter's amendment would fix that, while still ensuring that terrorists like Mohammed are swiftly brought to justice.

You are also going to hear a lot about how lawyers are going to file all kinds of frivolous lawsuits on behalf of detainees if habeas corpus is in place. This is a cynical argument because I think we could get overwhelming support in this Chamber right now for a measure that would restrict habeas to a one-shot appeal that would be limited solely to whether someone was legally detained or not.

I am not interested in allowing folks at Guantanamo to complain about whether their cell is too small or whether the food they get is sufficiently edible or to their tastes. That is not what this is about. We can craft a habeas bill that says the only question before the court is whether there is sufficient evidence to find that this person is truly an unlawful enemy combatant and belongs in this detention center. We can restrict it to that.

And although I have seen some of those amendments floating around, those were not amendments that were admitted during this debate. It is a problem that is easily addressed. It is not a reason for us to wholesale eliminate habeas corpus.

Finally, you will hear some Senators argue that if habeas is allowed, it renders the CSRT process irrelevant because the courts will embark on de novo review, meaning they will completely retry these cases, take new evidence. So whatever findings were made in the CSRT are not really relevant because the court is essentially going to start all over again.

I actually think some of these Senators are right on this point. I believe we could actually set up a system in which a military tribunal is sufficient to make a determination as to whether someone is an enemy combatant and would not require the sort of traditional habeas corpus that is called for as a consequence of this amendment—where the court's role is simply to see whether proper procedures were met.

The problem is that the way the CSRT is currently designed is so insufficient that we can anticipate the Supreme Court overturning this underlying bill, once again, in the absence of habeas corpus review.

I have had conversations with some of the sponsors of the underlying bill who say they agree that we have to beef up the CSRT procedures. Well, if we are going to revisit the CSRT procedures to make them stronger and make sure they comport with basic due process, why not leave habeas corpus in place until we have actually fixed it up to our satisfaction?

Why rush through it two days before we are supposed to adjourn? Because some on the other side of the aisle want to go campaign on the issue of who is tougher on terrorism and national security.

Since 9/11, Americans have been asked to give up certain conveniences and civil liberties—long waits in airport security lines, random questioning because of a foreign-sounding last name—so that the Government can defeat terrorism wherever it may exist. It is a tough balance to strike.

I think we have to acknowledge that whoever was in power right now, whoever was in the White House, whichever party was in control, that we would have to do some balancing between civil liberties and our need for security and to get tough on those who would do us harm.

Most of us have been willing to make some sacrifices because we know that, in the end, it helps to make us safer. But restricting somebody's right to challenge their imprisonment indefinitely is not going to make us safer. In fact, recent evidence shows it is probably making us less safe.

In Sunday's New York Times, it was reported that previous drafts of the recently released National Intelligence Estimate, a report of sixteen different Government intelligence agencies, describe:

"actions by the United States Government that were determined to have stoked the jihad movement, like the indefinite detention of prisoners at Guantanamo Bay."

This is not just unhelpful in our fight against terror, it is unnecessary. We don't need to imprison innocent people to win this war. For people who are guilty, we have the procedures in place to lock them up. That is who we are as a people. We do things right, and we do things fair.

Two days ago, every Member of this body received a letter, signed by thirty-five U.S. diplomats, many of whom served under Republican Presidents. They urged us to reconsider eliminating the rights of habeas corpus from this bill, saying:

"To deny habeas corpus to our detainees can be seen as a prescription for how the captured members of our own military, diplomatic, and NGO personnel stationed abroad may be treated.

The Congress has every duty to insure their protection, and to avoid anything which will be taken as a justification, even by the most disturbed minds, that arbitrary arrest is the acceptable norm of the day in the relations between nations, and that judicial inquiry is an antique, trivial and dispensable luxury."

The world is watching what we do today in America. They will know what we do here today, and they will treat all of us accordingly in the future—our soldiers, our diplomats, our journalists, anybody who travels beyond these borders. I hope we remember this as we go forward. I sincerely hope we can protect what has been called the "great writ"—a writ that has been in place in the Anglo-American legal system for over 700 years.

Mr. President, this should not be a difficult vote. I hope we pass this amendment because I think it is the only way to make sure this underlying bill preserves all the great traditions of our legal system and our way of life.

I yield the floor.

Martin Luther King Jr. Memorial

Groundbreaking Ceremony
November 13, 2006

I want to thank first of all the King family, we would not be here without them. I want to thank Mr. Johnson and the foundation for allowing me to share this day with all of you. I wish to recognize as well my colleagues in the United States Senate who have helped make today possible. Senators Paul Sarbanes and John Warner, who wrote the bill for this memorial. Senators Thad Cochran and Robert Byrd who appropriated the money to help build it. Thank you all.

I have two daughters, ages five and eight. And when I see the plans for this memorial, I think about what it will like when I first bring them here upon the memorial's completion. I imagine us walking down to this tidal basin, between one memorial dedicated to the man who helped give birth to a nation, and another dedicated to the man who preserved it. I picture us walking beneath the shadows cast by the Mountain of Despair, and gazing up at the Stone of Hope, and reading the quotes on the wall together as the water falls like rain.

And at some point, I know that one of my daughters will ask, perhaps my youngest, will ask, "Daddy, why is this monument here? What did this man do?"

How might I answer them? Unlike the others commemorated in this place, Dr. Martin Luther King Jr. was not a president of the United States—at no time in his life did he hold public office. He was not a hero of foreign wars. He never had much money, and while he lived he was reviled at least as much as

153

he was celebrated. By his own accounts, he was a man frequently racked with doubt, a man not without flaws, a man who, like Moses before him, more than once questioned why he had been chosen for so arduous a task—the task of leading a people to freedom, the task of healing the festering wounds of a nation's original sin.

And yet lead a nation he did. Through words, he gave voice to the voiceless. Through deeds, he gave courage to the faint of heart. By dint of vision, and determination, and most of all faith in the redeeming power of love—he endured the humiliation of arrest, the loneliness of a prison cell, the constant threats to his life, until he finally inspired a nation to transform itself, and begin to live up to the meaning of its creed.

Like Moses before him, he would never live to see the Promised Land. But from the mountain top, he pointed the way for us—a land no longer torn asunder with racial hatred and ethnic strife, a land that measured itself by how it treats the least of these, a land in which strength is defined not simply by the capacity to wage war but by the determination to forge peace—a land in which all of God's children might come together in a spirit of brotherhood.

We have not yet arrived at this longed for place. For all the progress we have made, there are times when the land of our dreams recedes from us—when we are lost, wandering spirits—content with our suspicions and our angers, our long-held grudges and petty disputes, our frantic diversions and tribal allegiances.

And yet, by erecting this monument, we are reminded that this different, better place beckons us, and that we will find it not across distant hills or within some hidden valley, but rather we will find it somewhere in our hearts.

In the Book of Micah, Chapter 6, verse 8, the prophet says that God has already told us what is good.

"What doth the Lord require of thee," the verse tells us, "but to do justly, and to love mercy, and to walk humbly with thy God?"

The man we honor today did what God required. In the end, that is what I will tell my daughters—I will leave it to their teachers and their history books to tell them the rest.

As Dr. King asked to be remembered, I will tell them that this man gave his life serving others. I will tell them that this man tried to love somebody. I will tell them that because he did these things, they live today with the freedom God intended, their citizenship unquestioned, their dreams unbounded. And I will tell them that they too can love. That they too can serve. And that each generation is beckoned anew, to fight for what is right, and strive for what is just, and to find within itself the spirit, the sense of purpose, that can remake a nation and transform a world.

Thank you very much.

Memorial Day Speech

Abraham Lincoln National Cemetery
Elwood, Illinois
May 30, 2005

Thank you for allowing me the honor of joining you here today.

This is my first time visiting the Abraham Lincoln National Cemetery, and as I was driving through I thought to myself that the staff and the volunteers who have made this possible should feel very proud of the work they're doing—this is a beautiful place for our veterans to come home to.

Among red maples and sturdy oaks, over 10,000 Americans now lay here, resting peacefully under an endless Illinois sky.

They rest in silence. On a typical day, except for scattered footsteps or the soft gurgling of a stream, I imagine you could walk row after row of headstones without hearing a single sound.

It isn't until you come across another visitor—a widow watering the plant she brought for her husband, a little girl planting a flag at her father's headstone, a mother shedding tears on the wreath she will lay for her son—that you realize something: In this place we have come to associate with the quiet of death, the memories of loved ones speak to us so strongly that when we stop and listen, we can't help but hear life.

And once a year on this day, in the fullness of spring, in the presence of those who never really leave us, it is life that we honor. Lives of courage, lives of sacrifice, and the ultimate measure of selflessness—lives that were given to save others.

What led these men and women to wear their country's uniform?

What is it that leads anyone to put aside their own pursuit of happiness, to subordinate their own sense of survival for something larger—something greater?

Behind each stone is one of these stories; a personal journey that eventually led to the decision to fight for one's country and defend the freedoms we enjoy. Most of the Americans who rest here were like my grandfather, a WWII vet who volunteered after Pearl Harbor, fought in Patton's Army, but was lucky enough to came back in one piece, and went on to live well into his twilight years.

My grandfather never boasted about it. He treated the fact that he served in the military like it was only a matter of fact.

And so it is easy for us to forget sometimes that, like my grandfather, the men and women resting here—whose service spans a century of conflict from the Civil War to the War in Iraq—chose their path at a very young age.

These were kids who went to war.

They had a whole life ahead of them—birthdays and weddings, holidays with children and grandchildren, homes and jobs and happiness of their own. And yet, at one moment or another, they felt the tug. Maybe it was a President's call to save the Union and to free the slaves. Maybe it was the day of

THE VOICE THAT CHANGED A NATION

infamy that awakened a nation to the dangers of Fascism. Or maybe it was the morning we saw our security disappear then the twin towers collapsed.

And at that moment, whatever the moment was, these men and women thought of a mom or a dad, a husband or a wife, or a child not yet born. They thought of a landscape, or a way of life, or a flag, or the words of freedom they'd learned to love. And they determined that it was time to go. They decided, "I must serve so that the people I love may live happily, safely, freely."

Oliver Wendell Holmes once remarked, "To fight out a war, you must believe something and want something with all your might."

The Americans who lay here believed.

And when they waved goodbye to their families—some for the last time—they held those beliefs close as they crossed the ocean towards an unknown destiny.

And they made us very proud.

No matter how many veterans you may meet, or how many stories of heroism you may hear, every encounter reminds you that through their service, these men and women have lived out the ideals that stir our Nation—honor, duty, sacrifice.

They're people like Seamus Ahern, who I met during the campaign at a V.F.W. hall in East Moline, Illinois. He told me about how he'd joined the Marines because his country had given so much to him, and he felt that as a young person he needed to give something back. We became friends and we kept in touch over email while he was in Iraq. One day he sent me an email that said, "I'm sorry I haven't written more often—I've been a little busy over here in Falujah." I had to reply, "I don't think it's necessary to apologize."

They're people like Major Tammy Duckworth, a helicopter pilot with the Illinois Army Guard. Four months ago, she lost both of her legs when a rocket was shot through the floor of her Black Hawk helicopter over Iraq. And yet, last month she came to the United States Senate to testify about ways we can improve the process of rehabilitating injured vets. And as we speak, she has already begun training so that she can fly again for her country one day.

They're the people I had the honor of meeting at Walter Reed Medical Center in Washington. Young men and women who may have lost limbs or broken their backs or severed their nerves, but have not lost the will to live or the pride they feel in having served their country. They have no time for self-pity, but wish only to recuperate as quickly as they can and meet the next challenge.

It is this quintessentially American optimism that stands out in our veterans. To meet these men and women gives you a clear sense of the quality of person we have serving in the United States Armed Forces.

No wonder, then, that when these men and women come home from war, they return to parades and salutes, the arms of loved ones, and the waving flags of children.

But today, on Memorial Day, we also remember that some come home in a different way. The news of their impending arrival is delivered with a soft knock on the door. Their return comes with the sound of a twenty-one gun salute and the lonely notes of taps.

THE VOICE THAT CHANGED A NATION

I won't pretend that simple words of condolence could ever ease the pain of the loss for the families they leave behind. I am the father of two little girls, and when I see the parents who have come here today to lay wreaths for the children they lost, my heart breaks with theirs.

But I will say to those parents that here in Illinois and all across America, other children and other parents look to your children and their service as a shining example of what's best in this land.

During the Civil War, President Lincoln took a moment to sit down and personally write a condolence letter to a Mrs. Bixby of Massachusetts after he had learned that she lost five of her sons in battle. In that letter, the President wrote:

"I pray that our Heavenly Father may assuage the anguish of your bereavement, and leave you only the cherished memory of the loved and lost, and the solemn pride that must be yours to have laid so costly a sacrifice upon the altar of freedom."

Here on this hallowed ground and in ceremonies across the nation, we choose this day to solemnly honor those costly sacrifices—sacrifices that were made on the fields of Gettysburg, the beaches of Normandy, the deserts of Iraq, and so many other distant lands. It makes our hearts heavy; our heads bow in respect.

But amid the quiet of this spring day in Elwood, we also hear life. And as we are called by the memories of those who found the courage to lay down a life so that others may live, we thank God for blessing us with the privilege of knowing such heroic sons and daughters of America.

161

On the Death of Rosa Parks

Senate Floor Statement
October 25, 2005

Mr. President, today the nation mourns a genuine American hero. Rosa Parks died yesterday in her home in Detroit. Through her courage and by her example, Rosa Parks helped lay the foundation for a country that could begin to live up to its creed.

Her life, and her brave actions, reminded each and every one of us of our personal responsibilities to stand up for what is right and the central truth of the American experience: that our greatness as a nation derives from seemingly ordinary people doing extraordinary things.

Rosa Parks' life was a lesson in perseverance. As a child, she grew up listening to the Ku Klux Klan ride by her house, and lying in bed at night fearing that her house would be burnt down. In her small hometown in Alabama, she attended a one-room school for African-American children that only went through the sixth grade. When she moved to Montgomery, Alabama, to continue her schooling, she was forced to clean classrooms after school to pay her tuition. Although she attended Alabama State Teachers College, Rosa Parks would later make her living as a seamstress and housekeeper.

But she didn't accept that her opportunities were limited to sewing clothes or cleaning houses. In her forties, Rosa Parks was appointed secretary of the Montgomery branch of the NAACP and was active in voter registration drives with the Montgomery Voters League. In the summer of 1955, she attended the Highlander Folk School, where she took classes in workers' rights and racial equality. Well before she made headlines across the country, she was a highly respected member of the Montgomery community and a committed member of the civil rights effort.

Of course, her name became permanently etched in American history on December 1, 1955, when she was arrested for refusing to give up her seat to a white passenger on a Montgomery bus. It wasn't the first time Rosa Parks refused to acquiesce to the Jim Crow system. The same bus driver who had her arrested had thrown her off a bus the year before for refusing to give up her seat.

Some schoolchildren are taught that Rosa Parks refused to give up her seat because her feet were tired. Our nation's schoolbooks are only getting it half right. She once said, "The only tired I was, was tired of giving in."

This solitary act of civil disobedience became a call to action. Her arrest led a then relatively unknown pastor, Martin Luther King, Jr., to organize a boycott of the Montgomery bus system. That boycott lasted 381 days and culminated in a landmark Supreme Court decision finding that the city's segregation policy was unconstitutional.

This solitary act of civil disobedience was also the spark that ignited the beginning of the end for segregation and inspired millions around the country and ultimately around the world to get involved in the fight for racial equality.

Rosa Parks' persistence and determination did not end that day in Montgomery, nor did it end with the passage of the Civil Rights Act and Voting Rights Act years later. She stayed active in the NAACP and other civil rights groups for years.

From 1965 to 1988, Ms. Parks continued her public service by working for my good friend, Congressman John Conyers. And in an example of her low-key demeanor, her job in Congressman Conyers' office did not involve appearances as a figurehead or celebrity; she helped homeless folks find housing.

At the age of 74, she opened the Rosa and Raymond Parks Institute for Self-Development, which offers education and job training programs for disadvantaged youth. And even into her 80s, Rosa Parks gave lectures and attended meetings with civil rights groups.

At the age of 86, Rosa Parks' courage and fortitude was recognized by President Bill Clinton, who awarded her the nation's highest honor for a civilian—the Congressional Gold Medal.

As we honor the life of Rosa Parks, we should not limit our commemorations to lofty eulogies. Instead, let us commit ourselves to carrying on her fight, one solitary act at a time, and ensure that her passion continues to inspire as it did a half-century ago. That, in my view, is how we can best thank her for her immense contributions to our country.

Rosa Parks once said, "As long as there is unemployment, war, crime, and all things that go to the infliction of man's inhumanity to man, regardless—there is much to be done, and people need to work together."

Now that she's passed, it's up to us to make sure that her message is shared. While we will miss her cherished spirit, let's work to ensure that her legacy lives on in the heart of the nation.

As a personal note, I think it is fair to say were it not for that quiet moment of courage by Mrs. Parks, I would not be standing here today. I owe her a great thanks, as does the Nation. She will be sorely missed.

Thank you. I yield the floor.

CPSIA information can be obtained
at www.ICGtesting.com
Printed in the USA
LVHW041139140119
603823LV00004B/743/P

9 780982 375655